*Beyond Survival*

# Beyond Survival
## Protecting Households from Health Shocks in Latin America

Cristian C. Baeza

Truman G. Packard

A COPUBLICATION OF STANFORD ECONOMICS AND FINANCE,
AN IMPRINT OF STANFORD UNIVERSITY PRESS, AND THE WORLD BANK

A copublication of Stanford Economics and Finance, an imprint of Stanford University Press, and the World Bank.

| Stanford University Press | The World Bank |
| --- | --- |
| 1450 Page Mill Road | 1818 H Street, NW |
| Palo Alto, Calif. 94304 | Washington, DC 20433 |

The findings, interpretations, and conclusions expressed herein are those of the author(s) and do not necessarily reflect the views of the Board of Executive Directors of the World Bank or the governments they represent.

The World Bank does not guarantee the accuracy of the data included in this work. The boundaries, colors, denominations, and other information shown on any map in this work do not imply any judgment on the part of the World Bank concerning the legal status of any territory or the endorsement or acceptance of such boundaries.

**Rights and Permissions**

| ISBN 10: 0-8213-6571-1 | (World Rights except North America) |
| --- | --- |
| ISBN 13: 978-0-8213-6571-7 | (World Rights except North America) |
| ISBN 0-8047-5674-0 (Hardcover) | (North America) |
| ISBN 0-8047-5675-9 (Softcover) | (North America) |
| eISBN: 0-8213-6572-X | |
| DOI: 10.1596/978-0-8213-6571-7 | |

*Library of Congress Cataloging-in-Publication Data has been requested.*

# Latin American Development Forum Series

This series was created in 2003 to promote, debate, and disseminate information and analysis and convey the excitement and complexity of the most topical issues in economic and social development in Latin America and the Caribbean. It is sponsored by the Inter-American Development Bank, the United Nations Economic Commission for Latin America and the Caribbean, and the World Bank. The manuscripts chosen for publication represent the highest quality in each institution's research and activity output and have been selected for their relevance to the academic community, policy makers, researchers, and interested readers.

## Advisory Committee Members

# Contents

# Foreword

Despite nearly two decades of bold structural reform in the health sector, households in the Latin America and Caribbean region are still overexposed to health shocks that can force them to cut consumption of other basic services and goods and even result in destitution. Around the world, including in Latin America, health care costs are rising. Health shocks—such as sickness, accidents, or normal life-cycle events like such as age—sap the health of individuals and can impoverish their households. Besides treatment costs, households bear the cost of productive time lost from work, as well as opportunity costs due to days spent taking care of ill family members. The combined costs and loss of income of a serious illness or injury can force individuals and households into poverty. For those who are already poor, these costs perpetuate poverty.

*Beyond Survival: Protecting Households from Health Shocks in Latin America* breaks new ground in the ongoing debate about health finance and financial protection from the costs of health care. This book reviews existing and new evidence on the mechanisms and magnitude of impoverishing effects of health events and the importance of public policy to prevent such impoverishment.

The evidence and discussion in *Beyond Survival* is intended to persuade policy makers to weigh both health status and financial protection objectives when setting priorities for their health systems. The balance struck between the two goals is ultimately a societal decision based mostly on country context and preferences. Low-income/high mortality countries will most likely focus on health status gains. Higher income countries, which in most cases in Latin America and the Caribbean have achieved important gains in the health status of the population, would be well advised to increase somewhat their focus on financial protection. Indeed, health shocks are one of the most frequent reasons for households in the lower-income quintiles, that are not already poor, to fall into poverty as a consequence of both high out-of-pocket expenditures and lost income.

Applying a classical insurance framework to examine household behavior in the face of health shocks, the authors conclude that Latin American households are over-burdened with out-of-pocket spending and lack sufficient risk pooling. Furthermore, social health insurance in the region—a prevalent form of risk pooling—too often covers all health events, regardless of their nature (that is, whether they are "insurable" or not). But since social health insurance covers all events, it cannot cover all households. The authors argue that if the instruments governments provide to help households manage the financial losses from health shocks were correctly aligned to the nature of those losses, health finance systems would be better able to provide fiscally *sustainable* financial protection to a greater share of the population. Correctly aligned instruments would free up resources to provide subsidies for people who cannot afford to pay for contributory forms of risk-pooling or illness-prevention activities.

Including the poor, those at high risk and especially the fast-growing group of self-employed and informal workers in effective health risk-pooling arrangements pose an awesome challenge for policy makers in Latin America. To meet this challenge in the current context—where contributory social insurance coexists with "noncontributory" national health services financed from general revenue in almost every Latin American country—policy makers will need differentiated strategies for three distinct household groups: the *nonpoor*, whose contribution capacity is above the average cost of the health benefits package for most or all of their life cycle; the *poor*, whose contribution capacity rarely reaches the average cost of the package at any time in their life cycle; and the *high risk*, whose contribution was above the average cost of the package for much of their lives but who reach an age (or health risk) for which the average cost of the package outstrips their capacity to contribute.

The authors conclude that the first step toward extending fiscally sustainable coverage against health shocks is to correctly define a *benefits package* of coverage of insurable health events. To provide effective financial protection, the package has to be concentrated around impoverishing events.

Once such a financially viable benefits package is defined, policy makers have several options to increase participation of self-employed and informal nonpoor workers: to facilitate—through regulation, innovations in enrollment practices, or both—participation in contributory health insurance; to improve enforcement of mandatory participation and strengthen evasion control; to increase the effectiveness of means testing for access to free, publicly subsidized health services; and to reduce the contribution–benefits gap.

Furthermore, the authors propose a challenging long-term reform agenda. Their long-term vision is a system in which contribution-benefits gaps are reduced through a combination of (1) delinking risk-pool financing from labor status; (2) reducing costs of participation in contributory health risk pooling, by, for example, unbundling participation in health insurance from other benefits that informal workers are unlikely to get; and (3) increasing the perceived benefits of participation (e.g., raising the quality of health services). Perhaps the most challenging part of such a proposed agenda refers to the delinking risk-pooling financing from labor market status, as it would imply gradually reducing and eventually replacing payroll-tax financing with financing from general tax revenue. Given their present fiscal weakness, for most Latin American countries such a shift would require important tax reforms over the long run and a highly complex transition.

Guillermo Perry
Chief Economist for Latin America and the Caribbean
The World Bank
June 2006

# Acknowledgments

THIS REGIONAL STUDY WAS PREPARED BY A TEAM LED BY CRISTIAN BAEZA (LCSHH) and Truman Packard (LCSHS), with special technical support from Fernando Montenegro Torres (LCSHH). Other members of the team included John L. Fiedler (LCSHH), Maria L. Escobar (LCSHH), Pablo Gottret (HDNHE), and Martha P. Vargas (LCSHD). The team benefited from valuable contributions from Ariel Fiszbein (LCSHD), Joe Kutzin (WHO/Euro), Alejandro Ferreiro (government of Chile), Jesus Maria Fernandez (LCSHH), Paul Gertler (HDNVP), April Harding (LCSHH), Theresa Jones (LCSHS), Andrew Mason (LCSHS), Alexander S. Preker (AFTH2), Luis Servén (DECRG), Helena Ribe (LCSHS), and Keith Hansen (LCSHH). Peer reviewers for this study were Indermit S. Gill (EASPR), George Schieber (HDNHE), Armin Fidler (ECSHD), and Marcelo Tokman (Ministry of Finance, Chile). Guillermo Perry is the chief economist for the Latin America and the Caribbean (LAC) region and Evangeline Javier is the sector director for the Human Development Department in LAC.

Ricardo Bitran & Associates (on Chile and Colombia); Daniel Maceira (on Argentina); Felicia Knaul, Hector Arreola, and Javier E. Suazo (on Mexico); Rahim Nazarali; Fernando Montenegro Torres (reviewing relevant literature, and on Ecuador); and John L. Fiedler (on Honduras) provided background papers for this study.

The authors are grateful for the guidance and recommendations provided by the participants in the regional consultation in Bogotá, Colombia, on June 27, 2005. The panel was composed of Pedro García Aspíllaga (Minister of Health, Chile); Ginés González García (Minister of Health and Environment, Argentina); Diego Palacio (Minister of Social Protection, Colombia); Marcelo Tokman (Chief of Economic Policy, Ministry of Finance, Chile); Eduardo González Pier (Chief of Economic Analysis, Health Secretariat, Mexico); Manuel Inostroza (Superintendent, Superintendency of Health, Chile); Daniel Olesker

(Director General, Ministry of Health, Uruguay); Roberto Cocheteux (President, Asociación Latinoamericana de Medicina Integral [ALAMI]); Leonardo Di Pietro (Chief of Cabinet, Ministry of Health and Environment, Argentina); Roberto Esguerra (Director, Fundación Santa Fe de Bogotá, Colombia); Hector Sanchez Rodrìguez (Executive Director, Institute of Public Policy and Health Management, Universidad Andrés Bello, Chile); Walter Valle (Policy Adviser, Ministry of Health and Environment, Argentina); and Hugh Waters (Assistant Professor, Johns Hopkins University, United States).

# About the Authors

**Cristian C. Baeza** is the lead health policy specialist in the Latin America and the Caribbean Region at the World Bank. His focus is health financing and health systems and their contribution to social protection and poverty alleviation.

He was the senior health systems specialist for Social Security Policy and Development at the International Labor Organization. Previously, he was founder and CEO of the Latin American Center for Health Systems Research (CLAISS) in Santiago, Chile; national director of the Chilean National Health Fund (FONASA); health systems specialist at the World Bank in Washington, D.C.; and chief of the International Financing Division and of the Health Sector Reform Program at the Chilean Ministry of Health.

Dr. Baeza is a medical doctor from the University of Chile and holds a Master of Public Health degree from Johns Hopkins University and a degree in economics of social policy from Instituto Latinoamericano de Doctrina y Estudios Sociales.

**Truman G. Packard** is a senior economist in the Latin America and the Caribbean Region at the World Bank. He began work on pensions in 1995, when he worked with World Bank staff in Mexico to develop adjustment operations needed to support pension reform. Since then he has participated in analytical and lending assistance to support both pension reform and broader efforts to strengthen social insurance. His research focuses on how pensions and social insurance affect the efficiency of labor markets and incentives to save. He holds a Ph.D. in economics from the University of Oxford.

# Abbreviations

| | |
|---|---|
| ADL | activities of daily living |
| ARS | Administradora de Régimen Subsidiado, Colombia |
| ASSE | State Health Service Administration, Uruguay |
| AUGE | Plan de Acceso Universal con Garantías Explícitas, Chile |
| BP | benefits package |
| CASES | Catálogo de Servicios Esenciales de Salud, Mexico |
| CASS | Caja Costarricense de Seguro Social |
| CEPAL | Comisión Económica para America Latina |
| CFPGC | Catálogo del Fondo de Protección contra Gastos Catastróficos, Mexico |
| CIF | comprehensive insurance framework |
| CLAISS | Centro Latinoamericano de Investigación de Sistemas de Salud |
| CLAS | Comites Locales de Administración de Salud |
| CMH | Commission on Macroeconomics and Health |
| CNSS | National Social Security Council, Colombia |
| CPB | Conjunto de Prestaciones Básicas, Argentina |
| DISSE | Dirección de Seguros Sociales por Enfermedad |
| DRG | Diagnostic Related Group |
| EPSs | Empresas Promotoras de Salud, Colombia |
| F&F | friends and family |
| FNR | Fondo Nacional de Recursos |
| FONASA | Fondo Nacional de Salud, Chile |
| FOSYGA | Solidarity Fund, Colombia |
| GDP | gross domestic product |
| GP | general practitioner |
| GPFH | GP Fund Holders, United Kingdom |
| GT | general taxation |
| HA | Health Authority (regional), United Kingdom |
| HH | households |

| | |
|---|---|
| IAMC | Mutual Health Insurance Organization |
| IDSS | Instituto Dominicano de Seguridad Social |
| IESS | Instituto Ecuatoriano de Seguridad Social |
| IHSS | Instituto Hondureño de Seguridad Social |
| ILO | International Labor Organization/Office |
| IMSS | Instituto Mexicano de Seguridad Social |
| ISAPRE | Instituciones de Salud Previsional, Chile |
| ISSSTE | Instituto de Seguridad y Servicios Sociales para los Trabajadores del Estado, Mexico |
| LAC | Latin America and the Caribbean |
| LIC | low-income country |
| MIC | middle-income country |
| MOH | ministry of health |
| NHS | national health service |
| OOP | out-of-pocket |
| OSN | Obras Sociales Nacionales, Argentina |
| PAHO | Pan American Health Organization |
| PAMI | Instituto Nacional de Servicios Sociales para Jubilados y Pensionados, Argentina |
| PCG | Primary Care Groups, United Kingdom |
| PMO | Plan Medico Obligatorio, Argentina |
| POS | Plan Obligatorio de Salud, Colombia |
| PPP | purchasing power parity |
| PRIESO | Encuesta de Previsión de Riesgos Sociales, Chile and Peru |
| PRT | payroll tax |
| SI | social insurance |
| SILAIS | Local Integrated Health Care System, Nicaragua |
| SIS | Integrated Health Insurance, Peru |
| SNHS | Spanish National Health System |
| SPS | Seguro Popular de Salud |
| SS | social security |
| SSC | Farmer's Insurance, Ecuador |
| STEP | Strategies and Tools against Social Exclusion and Poverty, ILO |
| VAT | value added tax |
| WHO | World Health Organization |

# Executive Summary

*Beyond Survival: Protecting Households from Health Shocks in Latin America* breaks new ground in the ongoing debate about health finance and financial protection from the costs of health care. It is based on a review of the little that has been written on the topic of financial protection and the risk of poverty from health shocks, and on empirical evidence from six case studies commissioned for this report: Argentina, Chile, Colombia, Ecuador, Honduras, and Mexico (published separately). Financial protection is defined as protecting households from impoverishment as a result of health shocks.

For policy makers in Latin America and the Caribbean (LAC), *Beyond Survival* carries five main messages:

• Health care costs—insurance contributions as well as out-of-pocket payments—and loss of income as a consequence of sickness can impoverish households and plunge the already poor into a transgenerational cycle of abject poverty. This reflects a lack of access to effective instruments for income protection during sickness, and protection from the risks of catastrophic health costs, risk pooling. It is manifested in the disproportionately high part of average income and health care costs financed out-of-pocket in the LAC region relative to other parts of the world.

• People need protection from the potentially ruinous costs of health care and loss of income due to sickness. These costs rival losses of income from unemployment as a cause of poverty.

• The focus of risk pooling in LAC has been mostly on formally employed, salaried workers who are covered by mandatory public and quasi-public risk-pooling mechanisms. As long as this situation persists, governments in LAC will be hard pressed to ensure effective coverage beyond this comparatively well-off minority.

• The constitutions of most LAC countries recognize citizens' basic right to health, but say little about the means of enforcing this right. Health care coverage can be expanded through increasing participation in risk pooling, by defining universal explicit rights to a benefits package (BP) of specified insurable events, and by better targeting subsidies to public health goods (such as vaccinations) to the poor, the aged, the indigent, and other disadvantaged groups.

*1*

- Extending risk pooling to the large and growing informal labor sector is a priority in LAC. This means inventing contribution mechanisms for nonpoor households to participate in risk pooling that are not linked to work place or labor status.

FROM A PUBLIC POLICY POINT OF VIEW, the relative priority given to gains in health status and to financial protection will vary with each country's individual circumstances. Returns from health-enhancing interventions are much different in poorer countries with low life expectancy and tight resources that are still seeking sufficient *breadth* of coverage, than in middle-income countries with long life expectancy that are increasingly focused on the *depth* of coverage. Breadth of coverage refers to the number of people that have access to basic services. Depth of coverage refers to the quality of the health benefits package—the number of interventions included and the technical characteristics of their delivery.

The balance struck between health status and financial protection is ultimately a societal decision based mostly on country context and preferences. The evidence and discussion in *Beyond Survival* is intended to persuade policy makers to weigh both health status and financial protection objectives when setting priorities for their health systems.

## Health Care Systems in LAC: Functions and Organization

A country's health care system encompasses all activities for which the primary objective is to improve, maintain, or restore the health of an individual or a population. Health service delivery, resource (inputs) generation, stewardship, and health financing are the four main health system functions.

Health system financing includes collecting and allocating revenue (sources) and managing financial risk. The traditional vehicle for managing financial risk is *risk pooling*. This means collecting and managing financial resources in a way that spreads risks and liabilities from the individual to all pool members, thus protecting individuals against catastrophic expenses. Financial risk pooling to protect individuals and households is the core function of health insurance mechanisms and has a preeminent focus in this report given its importance in protecting households against impoverishing health expenditures.

## Health Shocks, Household Welfare, and the Risk of Poverty

Around the world, health care costs are rising. *Health shocks*—adverse health events such as sickness, accidents, or normal life-cycle events such

*Figure ES.1* Percentage of Nonpoor Population Falling Below
        the National Poverty Line Due to Out-of-Pocket
        Health Expenditures

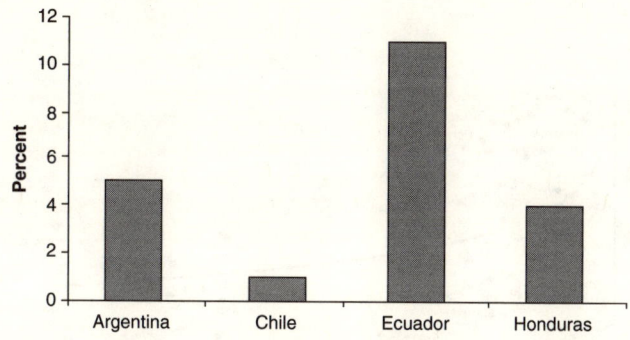

Source: Argentina, Maceira 2004; Chile, Bitran, Giedion, and Muñoz 2004;
Ecuador, Montenegro 2004; and Honduras, Fiedler 2004.

as old age—sap the health of individuals and can impoverish their
households. Besides treatment costs, households bear the cost of productive time lost from work, as well as opportunity costs due to days
spent taking care of ill family members. The combined costs and loss of
income for a serious illness or injury can force individuals and households to cut nonmedical consumption. For the already poor, these costs
perpetuate poverty.

For example, our case study results show that in Argentina, 5 percent
of all nonpoor households fell below the national poverty line for at least
three months in 1997 as a result of health spending. Similar outcomes
were observed in Chile (1 percent in 2000), Ecuador (11 percent in
2000), and Honduras (4 percent in 2000) (figure ES 1).

With total health expenditures accounting for 6.4 percent of gross domestic product (GDP), LAC is the highest-expending region in the world
after the countries in the Organisation for Economic Co-operation and
Development (OECD). Public expenditures on health are low in most
LAC countries, and private health expenditures correspondingly high.
As a percentage of per capita income, LAC countries have one of the
highest health spending ratios in the world (figure ES 2). By far, most
private health spending in the LAC region comes directly out-of-pocket
the moment public or private health services are sought.

*Figure ES.2* Average Total Annual per Capita Out-of-Pocket
Health Expenditures as a Percentage of Total
Annual Average per Capita Household
Consumption

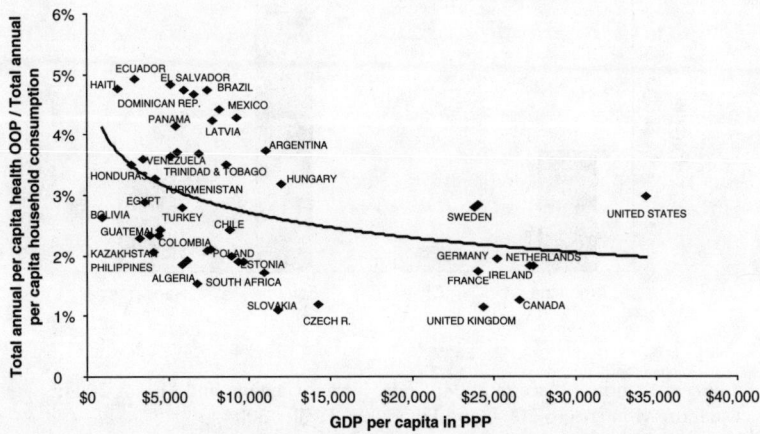

*Source:* Authors with data from WHO Country Data 2004 and World
Development Indicators 2003.

Households, especially the poorest, pay out-of-pocket for an unexpectedly high 85 percent of private health spending (as compared with
the 72 percent average in Europe and the OECD, which in addition have
much lower private expenditures in health). Notable exceptions to this
are Colombia and Uruguay. For households in the lower-income quintiles that are not already poor, the likelihood of falling into poverty
because of out-of-pocket health expenditures is greatest. Although
participation in well-designed and well-functioning risk-pooling
schemes reduces the likelihood of falling into poverty in the wake of a
health shock, few, if any, of the poor and near-poor participate in effective risk pooling.

All industrial countries have public policies providing for illness and
maternity leave to compensate for short-term, health-related income
loss, and private insurance (accidents or disability) or social security
cover longer medical leave and access to health services. Most LAC
countries have introduced these mechanisms for formal workers as part
of social security benefits. Households in every country we examined

can—at the very least—count on national health services delivered directly by national ministries of health.

Why then do health shocks drive LAC households into poverty when they are supposed to be covered by social health insurance or national health care and health finance arrangements provided directly by governments? What is failing or missing in LAC health systems? This report attempts to answer these questions through the deployment of theoretical tools, critical analysis of health sector reforms, and new empirical evidence.

Policy makers can recognize from the preliminary evidence presented in this report that data collection from households must be improved. Filling in blanks and refining data will allow further analysis of health system performance and financial protection for households still too exposed to health shocks. Study of the long-term effects on human capital formation in these vulnerable households should also be made a policy priority.

## Public Policy's Role in Household Protection against Health Shocks

Today, despite nearly two decades of bold structural reform in the health sector in many countries, households in LAC countries are still overexposed to health shocks that can force them to cut consumption of other basic services and goods and even result in destitution. To examine individual and household options, incentives, and likely choices to mitigate the financial impact of adverse health events, we found helpful the classical microeconomic insurance model used to study other income shocks.

In classical theory, individuals facing the likelihood of financial loss from an adverse event can either insure against such a loss or take steps to lower the likelihood the loss will occur. To mitigate the loss, they need to determine the optimal expenditure on alternative instruments—market insurance, self-insurance, and self-protection. The critical difference between the two insurance instruments is that market insurance functions by *pooling* risk across individuals; self-insurance—essentially individual saving—does not. The third mitigation instrument, self-protection or prevention, reduces the occurrence probability of the bad state, but because it does not transfer income from good to bad states, it does not affect the size of the loss if the bad state occurs. For simplicity, we refer to market insurance as risk pooling, to self-insurance as saving, and self-protection as prevention.

Using this framework, we conclude that LAC shows overreliance on out-of-pocket spending on health and lacks sufficient risk pooling. But we also conclude that social health insurance too often covers all health events, regardless of their nature (that is, whether they are insurable or not). If the instruments government provides to help households manage the financial losses from health shocks were correctly aligned to the nature of those losses, health finance systems would be better able to provide sustainable financial protection. Moreover, correctly aligned instruments might free up resources that would allow policy makers to finance subsidies to people who cannot afford to pay for contributory forms of risk pooling or illness-prevention activities and have no money left to save after paying for food, shelter, and other basic necessities. The amount of resources that correct alignment might make available is an empirical question for each country to answer and might vary greatly depending on each country's current social insurance entitlements.

POLICY MAKERS as well as households have alternative options for protection against the potential losses from a health shock: prevention, saving, and risk pooling. Risk pooling is a common public policy intervention. Risk pooling is most effectively used to cover treatment of relatively rare but costly health events. Considering the distribution and composition of household spending on health care in LAC, better alignment of the full array of instruments would allow risk-pooling coverage to be extended to lower-income and to already-poor households.

## The Role of Alternative Risk-Pooling Arrangements

Risk pooling is an essential tool for helping households and policy makers mitigate the financial effects of health shocks, thus lowering the risk of poverty.

Countries use different types of risk-pooling arrangements (figure ES 3). In LAC, risk pooling is most frequently organized under social insurance (SI) on the 19th century Bismarck model, with contributions linked to salaries, and on the national health service (NHS) or Beveridge model of the 1940s, usually financed from general taxation. Other risk-pooling arrangements include private, voluntary, and community-based health insurance—usually financed from contributions related to household health risk. Voluntary and community health insurance is less prevalent in LAC than SI or NHS.

The internal functional characteristics of risk pooling, more than the specific pooling arrangements, determine its effectiveness as a risk-protection tool. The preliminary evidence on the likely determinants of performance emerges from the LAC region's considerable experience

*Figure ES.3* Alternative Risk-Pooling Arrangements

In practice, countries use different
organizational arrangements for risk pooling

MOH/NHS

Insurance
schemes

Community
risk-
sharing
arrangements

Social
insurance

Multiple
competing private
insurance

Single    Multiple    Indemnity    Managed
care

MOH=ministry of health; NHS=national health service.
*Source:* Authors.

administering and reforming pooling structures, the almost exclusive focus of recent structural reform efforts in the health sector.

POLICY MAKERS could interpret this experience as suggesting that no matter what specific risk-pooling arrangement they choose, success in improving health status and financial protection for the population hinges on the way key health financing functions are implemented.

In addition to providing enough funding to run the health care system, ensuring that a health system provides financial protection requires:

• Achieving the highest possible contribution for insurable health events before services are needed (prepayment). This should help decrease out-of-pocket payments (the contribution at the moment services are needed), even with the use of copayments when necessary in the presence of proven signs of overuse of services.

• Achieving the largest possible risk pool within a population, or at least sufficiently large for financial viability and economies of scale. This should allow transfer of subsidies from lower-risk to higher-risk individuals (*risk subsidy*).

• Achieving adequate equity to ensure a reasonable flow of subsidies between higher-income groups to lower-income groups (*equity subsidization*).

• Developing purchasing capacity and a provider-payment system that creates incentives for providers to deliver quality health services in a timely manner while keeping costs down (*strategic purchasing*).

Previous evidence has been scarce on which alternative risk-pooling arrangements offer the best financial protection. Preliminary evidence from the case studies on Chile and Colombia suggests that differences among organizational arrangements are less important than the characteristics and composition of the benefits package (BP), the extent of strategic purchasing by the risk-pooling organization, the size of the pool, and the availability and size of equity subsidies. Risk-pool fragmentation and the regulatory framework for risk-pooling organizations also play an important role.

The BP lists the interventions covered; defines quality of service and its timing; sets copayments, deductibles (if any), and stop-loss provisions; and contains provisions on confidentiality, accommodations, privacy, access to patient information, patient rights, and other elements essential to the preservation of dignity. To provide effective financial protection, the package has to be concentrated around impoverishing events.

Through strategic purchasing, risk-pooling organizations create the right incentives for health care providers to deliver the BP-defined services and to monitor, verify, and enforce the BP conditions. This is the way most risk-pooling organizations (purchasers) use collected and pooled financial resources to buy health care services for their members.

Insufficient equity subsidies are an evident problem in low-income countries in the LAC region. Lack of resources explains most of the problem, but inefficient management of collected funds also contributes. Poverty and institutional and organizational instability inhibit adequate generation and collection of funds for an equity subsidy. The other cause of poor equity-subsidy performance is inefficient management or ineffective mechanisms for allocating the subsidy. A major distortion in the allocation mechanism is lack of portability, meaning that equity subsidies do not follow individuals changing from one risk pool (or job) to another.

We identify in the report growing inconsistencies between payroll tax–financed SI and the functioning of Latin America's labor markets. However, solving these inconsistencies will take time and in the short run it may be more important (and more feasible) to introduce changes in purchasing, pool size, and regulations governing existing arrangements than to attempt rapid shifts from one type of arrangement to another.

POLICY MAKERS in LAC need to dwell less on which risk-pooling arrangement they should pursue and concentrate much more on how the specifics of the financing functions work to improve people's health status and protect them financially. The sources, risk pooling, and volume of financing largely determine the system's capacity to achieve these goals. But for a given level of resources, it is vital to set a clear benefits package, implement strategic purchasing, and efficiently allocate risk and equity subsidies.

## Risk Pooling for Everyone: The Challenge of a Growing Informal Economy

Including the poor, the high-risk, and especially the fast-growing group of self-employed and informal workers in effective health risk-pooling arrangements poses an awesome challenge for policy makers in the LAC region. To meet it in the current context, where contributory social insurance coexists with national health services in almost every LAC country, policy makers will need differentiated strategies for three population groups:

- *The nonpoor:* individuals whose contribution capacity is above the average cost of the health BP for their entire life cycle
- *The poor:* individuals whose contribution capacity never reaches the average cost of the package at any time in their life cycle
- *The high-risk:* individuals whose contribution capacity was above the average cost of the package for much of their lives, but who reach an age (or health risk) for which the average cost of the package outstrips their capacity to contribute.

These distinctions are less relevant when risk pooling is organized as a single pool and with substantial or full financing from general taxation (for example, NHS). In these systems, risk-pool financing occurs at the societal level, and every member of society, at least in theory, has access to the same package of services independent of their contributions. Under these systems, fiscal sustainability is the challenge, which explains why many countries have no option but a mixed system combining NHS and contributory risk-pooling arrangements. However, distinguishing among these three populations becomes essential for health policy formulation in countries where governments choose (or where fiscal constraints leave them no other option) to organize risk pooling through contributory health insurance (social or private) or through a combination of contributory and noncontributory systems. Most LAC countries have chosen the mixed system.

Most policy challenges regarding inclusion of the poor in risk pooling are related to public subsidy policy, particularly efficiency and targeting (discussed in chapter 6). In contrast, the policy issues regarding the high-risk population are more closely related to old-age income security, including pensions. The challenges of including these two populations, but especially the poor, vary significantly among countries in the region. While publicly subsidized risk-pooling coverage is required for only 20 percent of the population in Chile, it is needed for more than 63 percent of the population in Bolivia and 50 percent in Honduras.[1]

Setting the correct participation incentives for self-employed and informal workers has proven extremely difficult. Their incomes are unobservable, their participation is entirely voluntary, and they have access to free health services from public providers. Why pay when good medical care can be had for free? This situation is compounded by the contribution-benefits gap, preordained by the contribution design, linked to payroll taxes and salary rather than risk. This design feeds incentives for adverse selection and results in nonparticipation by people who think their risk of ill health is much lower than implied by the requisite contribution.

---

POLICY MAKERS have four nonmutually exclusive options to increase participation of self-employed and informal nonpoor workers
1. Facilitate—through regulation or innovations in enrollment practices, or both—participation in contributory health insurance
2. Improve enforcement of mandatory participation and strengthen evasion control
3. Increase the effectiveness of means testing for access to free, publicly subsidized health services
4. Reduce the contribution-benefits gap.

---

The contribution-benefits gap can be reduced by: delinking risk-pool financing from labor status, shifting away from the use of payroll taxes, reducing perceived costs (contribution) of participation in contributory risk pooling (for example, unbundling participation in health insurance from other benefits that informal workers are unlikely to get), and increasing the perceived benefits of participation (for example, raising the quality of health services).

The best but hardest way would be delinking by gradually reducing and eventually replacing payroll tax–financing with financing from general tax revenue. For most LAC countries, this shift would mean important tax reforms over the long run and a complex transition.

Policy makers would therefore need to explore the short-term alternatives.

A note of caution is in order. The payroll tax is but one of myriad factors that add to the cost of formalization for workers and prospective employers, although the body of theoretical literature and empirical evidence showing the *negative* impact of high payroll tax contributions or a wide gap between contributions and perceived benefits on household incentives to participate in social insurance is large. Debate is also ongoing regarding how much the contribution-benefits gap influences a household's decision to join the formal labor market relative to other determinants, such as labor regulation or tax policy. SI for health risks and the wider social protection system is embedded deeply within the regulatory framework of a country's product and factor markets. In many countries, the decision to insure cannot be divorced from the decision to comply with regulations and taxation that have nothing to do with covering the risks to household welfare from health shocks or other adverse events.

POLICY MAKERS in each country need to assess the importance of payroll taxes and the contribution-benefits gap on self-employed and informal workers' decisions to participate, or not, in contributory risk pooling. The assessment may result in a decision to delink risk-pooling financing from labor status. However, they must be mindful, that this is but one of many worker and employer costs of formalization, which includes other taxes and labor regulations.

## The Quest for Efficiency and Universal Coverage: Health Sector Reform in LAC

The quest for universal coverage and improved efficiency of health systems has dominated LAC reform agendas for two decades. Most countries have attempted major reforms, mainly in revenue collection, risk pooling (including health insurance), and purchasing, but some have also attempted organizational reforms of public health service providers. Several governments have succeeded in implementing these reforms, while many have not yet met their objectives.

Reforms to delink health system financing from labor market status and to unbundle health insurance from pension mandates (discussed in chapter 5) are absent from the reform agenda. No country in the region has yet launched a delinking or an unbundling reform. Implementing either of the two, particularly delinking, would entail overcoming significant political tensions in the country.

## Lessons

So far, there is little evidence of the impact of health sector reforms on health status, use of services, or financial protection in LAC. However, evidence beginning to emerge suggests some lessons from health system reform and efforts to improve financial protection through universal risk pooling. These lessons are closely interrelated:

*Fiscal sustainability is all important.* Fiscal sustainability is crucial not only for a transition toward extending effective risk pooling to the entire population, particularly to the self-employed and the informal sector, but also for sustaining the gains of the last two decades. Transitioning away from payroll tax and toward increasing the share of health services financed from general tax revenue, if chosen by policy makers, will take a long time due to lagging tax-collection capacity and the complexity of pending tax reforms.

Fiscal sustainability constraints essentially mean "living within your means." For this, public sector tax revenue performance identifies only one part of the budget constraint. The other two parts have to do with the priority that governments give to the health sector for their resource allocation decisions and with the efficiency of the health system. While public sector tax revenue performance has more to do with the overall economic and fiscal context of a country and is "beyond the health sector," both public policy regarding priority of fiscal allocations to the health sector and reforms to improve the efficiency in the health system are clearly decisions that governments make, either explicitly or implicitly. Given existing fiscal sustainability constraints during the transition in most developing countries, worker participation in contributory risk pooling needs to be expanded and efficiency increased in the delivery of publicly financed health services. The LAC experience shows that changing the incentive framework for public providers and improving private sector participation are the roots of efficiency gains.

*For efficiency gains, it is essential to strengthen the purchasing-provider compact and increase provider autonomy in health personnel management to ensure improvement in the public provider incentive-performance framework and civil service reform.* Current supply-side financing, based mostly on past budget expenditures, sets perverse incentives within the public health sector. Even worse, it virtually determines that public providers will capture public subsidies and allows policy makers little or no flexibility for reallocating resources to fit current and emerging epidemiological and financial protection needs. This capture also makes contracting out to private providers, as needed, all but impossible, even when adequate public financing and regulatory frameworks are available.

Both improving the incentive framework for public providers and improving private sector participation in health care require strengthening of strategic purchasing, particularly by introducing provider-payment mechanisms linked to the production of services rather than to historical budgets. This new provider-payment system is a prerequisite for a transition away from historical supply-side financing toward demand-side, or production-based, payment mechanisms for public providers: "Money needs to follow the patient."

A well-designed financing system would send public providers the right price signals and incentives to improve technical efficiency, increase productivity, and improve responsiveness to consumers. However, a resounding lesson of provider-payment reform in LAC is that public providers need flexibility to manage all production factors. They have to be able to adapt their service production functions and cost structures to respond to continuously evolving price signals determined by the new payment mechanisms so that they can respond effectively to the ever changing needs of the population.

The average public provider in LAC spends 60 percent or more of its budgets on salaries, which makes human resources the prime production factor in health care delivery. Managers therefore need flexibility to allocate, hire, and fire their employees. To be successful, provider-payment reforms need to allow managers some autonomy to manage personnel as well as solve other traditional public ownership constraints on effective management.

*Private sector participation needs to be expanded in the delivery of publicly financed health services as well as contributory risk pooling.* This lack of flexibility largely explains concerns about the potential fiscal impact of increasing public purchasing from private providers. Chile's experience with Fondo Nacional de Salud and Colombia's experience with the Administradora de Régimen Subsidiado at the state level deserve close examination. In the absence of incremental resources, shifting away from supply-side historical financing for public providers, using part of the budget to purchase from private providers, or funding other public providers might generate deficits for public providers that lose revenue to their competitors. Even marginal deficits can unleash large disruptions. This would occur if the facility managers remain subject to rigid civil servant regulations for managing personnel that prevent them from adjusting the cost structure dynamically when demand for services slackens. Under such restrictions, deficits can occur.

Who ends up covering the deficits? Most likely the treasury (ministry of finance). Without flexibility to cut personnel costs to compensate for reduced revenue from the public purchaser, the public provider would have the same cost structure and would still have to pay people who cannot be transferred, laid off, or in some cases, not even retrained.

The initial provider-payment reforms and the increased selectivity of public purchasers in LAC have assumed that:

- Managers of public providers would receive and understand the price signals in the new payment mechanisms
- Managers would know how to respond and would act appropriately
- Managers would have the flexible, legal, and administrative environment allowing them to make the right changes
- Political authorities and the government would deal with the political problems associated with such flexibility.

Lessons from reform efforts in the LAC region have challenged all these assumptions.

## Challenges

Reforms to improve fiscal sustainability and public provider performance face three main challenges: covering the growing numbers of informal sector workers, negotiating the political constraints on health sector reform, and strengthening technical and institutional capacity for complex and time-extensive reforms. Improving private sector participation also faces the challenge of technical and institutional capacity, but its success is closely linked to fiscal sustainability and changing the incentive framework for public providers.

Vested interests can act as a formidable obstacle to efforts to improve the incentive framework for public providers and expand private sector participation. The introduction of labor flexibility and performance payments is rarely supported by health sector unions, usually the largest and most powerful public sector unions remaining after privatization of most public enterprises. For their part, influential private sector actors often interpret improvement of private sector participation as doing more of the same (much more). Improving private participation, does mean doing more, but it also means enacting and enforcing effective regulation for private insurers and private providers—rarely supported by owners of private sector providers. Moreover, discussion of both issues is highly ideological and politicized. Reformers, with rare exceptions, have found these two challenges difficult to surmount.

POLICY MAKERS need to clearly link the desired reforms to gains for ordinary people, not only for political accountability purposes, but also to ensure buy-in and support from voters who may otherwise side with powerful interest groups.

Health sector reforms in LAC are technically and institutionally demanding, and many of them are at the cutting edge of worldwide technical knowledge. This, coupled with a possible lack of in-country technical expertise and reform team continuity, poses momentous challenges.

POLICY MAKERS, from one administration to the next, need to make health sector reform a continuous, national policy, if it is to succeed. Continuity in reform policy and execution has proven essential.

# 1

# Health Care Systems in Latin America and the Caribbean: Functions and Organization

A COUNTRY'S HEALTH care system encompasses all activities to improve, maintain, or restore the health of an individual or a population (WHO 2000). Policy makers throughout Latin America and the Caribbean (LAC) have many options for financing and organizing their health systems. Their choices affect their success or failure in giving their people access to health services and protecting them from financial ruin as a result of costly illnesses—health shocks.

This chapter introduces readers to the key functions of health care systems, particularly health financing, which are discussed and analyzed in the ensuing chapters. The chapter also reviews how health systems are organized in the LAC region, identifies the subsidies households need at different times in their life cycle, presents the role and characteristics of risk pooling in facilitating these subsidies, and shows the importance of a defined benefits package (BP) of health services to the formulation of sound household subsidization policies.[1]

## Health System Functions

Health service delivery, resource (inputs) generation, stewardship, and health financing are the four main health system functions. Because financial protection is the main focus of this report, we concentrate on health system financing in this first chapter.

*Health service delivery* is the function that households are most familiar with—so much so that people often equate hospitals and other health service providers with the entire health system. Public and private service provision are the most visible products of the health system, for instance, inhospital care for chronically sick or injured patients, or ambulatory care for diabetics. The best systems also promote health and try to head-off illness and disease through education and preventive measures such as well-child consultations and vaccinations. To cushion people against the costs of the almost inevitable accidents and illnesses over a life time, effective health care systems have insurance and other income-protective mechanisms. All of these roles and activities mean that the system has to perform a wide range of activities. Delivering health services is thus an essential part of what the system *does*—but it is not what the system *is* (WHO 2000).

*Resource generation* is the function of assembling essential resources for delivering health services, but these inputs are usually produced at the fringes of the health system. These inputs include human resources (produced mostly by the education system with some input from the health system), medications, and medical equipment. Producing these resources often takes a long time (for example, a trained medical doctor, a new vaccine or drug). This function is often neglected or outside the immediate control of health system policy makers who, nevertheless, have to respond to short-term population needs with whatever resources are available.

*Stewardship* is the function of guiding key short- and long-term policy decisions to run the health system. This function is usually (but not always) a government responsibility. What are the health priorities to which public resources should be targeted? What is the institutional framework in which the system and its many actors should function? Which activities should be coordinated with other systems outside the realm of health care and how (for example, highway safety and food quality control)? What are the trends in health priorities and resource generation and their implications for the next 10, 20, or 30 years? What information is needed and by whom to ensure effective decision making on health matters? These questions are the core of the stewardship function.

*Health system financing* includes collecting, pooling, and allocating revenue (sources) and managing financial risk. In health system jargon, these functions are usually known, respectively, as funding or revenue collection, risk pooling, and purchasing. We briefly examine them all in this chapter.

The revenue collection function is a set of mechanisms by which the system or parts of the system assemble financial resources that will be pooled to pay for health care services. Revenue collection mechanisms are general taxation, mandatory payroll contributions, mandatory or voluntary risk-rated contributions (premiums), direct out-of-pocket expenditures, and other forms of personal savings. Each method of revenue collection is associated with a specific way of organizing and pooling funds and buying services. National health services (NHSs) are typically financed through general taxation. Social security organizations are usually financed through mandatory contributions from workers and employers (payroll contributions). Risk-rated premiums are typically associated with voluntary health insurance systems. Recent reforms, however, are changing these typical associations. For example, in Costa Rica a substantial part of the social security system is financed by allocations from general tax revenues in addition to payroll contributions (PAHO 2002). This is similar to Chile, where the national health care fund finances care for indigent groups (Fondo Nacional de Salud—FONASA) (Baeza and Copetta 1999), and Colombia finances most of its subsidized regime (Administradora de Régimen Subsidiado) (Baeza and Cabezas 1998).

Mechanisms used to collect resources include general tax contributions, salary-related contributions (payroll-tax), risk-related contributions (usually known as premiums) and diverse out-of-pocket payments made at the point of service (e.g., co-payments, user fees). The money households contribute in advance, before demanding the services, is generally known as prepayment. Low prepayments mean high out-of-pocket expanditures. High out-of-pocket payments can curtail access to health services and reduce financial protection.

*Risk pooling* refers to the collection and management of financial resources in a way that spreads financial risks from an individual to all pool members. Financial risk pooling is the core function of health insurance mechanisms.

From a policy perspective, risk-pooling arrangements attempt to manage the need to subsidize care for people with the highest health risks, the lowest ability to pay, or both, when facing a health shock.

Figure 1.1 illustrates the average individual's need for health care subsidies along his or her life cycle. It presents the evolution of the average cost of financing a set package of health services, her capacity to pay, and her need for subsidies at different times of life. The solid line shows the relation between actual average costs and age. The dotted line represents the relation between the individual's age and capacity to pay for the services. *Capacity to pay* is understood as the contribution amount that would not plunge the individual into poverty and thus prevent purchases of other vital services and goods. Because the risk of requiring health care services increases with age, it may exceed an individual's capacity to pay.

At point "A" in the figure, the individual (or household) would not need a subsidy to pay for the package. To the right of this point, the individual needs a subsidy to finance and gain access to needed services without incurring a ruinous expenditure or contribution. Higher-income households and individuals may never reach this point. But lower-income people may need a subsidy from birth for access to health care services society deems to be basic.

The need for subsidies can be satisfied by various mechanisms. A good financial protection health policy matches the subsidization

*Figure 1.1* The Cost of Health Services and Need for
Subsidization throughout the Life Cycle

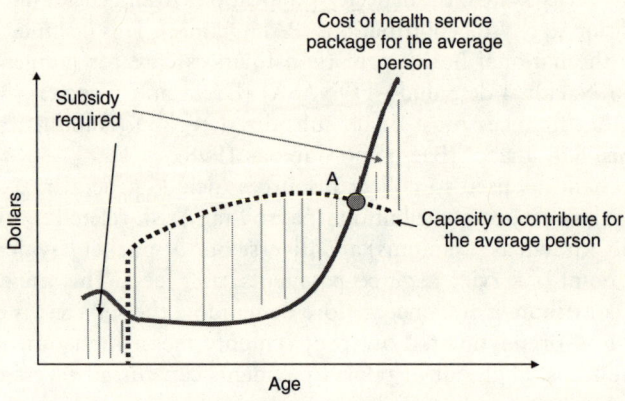

*Source:* Baeza et al. 2002, 23. Reproduced by permission.

mechanisms to the intervention triggering the need. This means identi-
fying the most appropriate mechanisms considering the uncertain nature
of the event and the size of the losses the event will cause. Most households solve the need for subsidies arising from small, certain events
through intrahousehold cross-subsidization. Savings are another possibility (an intertemporal cross-subsidy of a sort). However, because
any mishap further impoverishes very poor households, continuous
subsidies are needed for their financial protection.

Risk pooling plays a central role in facilitating cross-subsidization between low-risk and high-risk individuals, households, and communities.
By exploiting economies of scale, risk pooling can reduce the average
cost of the package, delaying the time an individual reaches "A." In contrast, without a system for spreading risk, high and unexpected out-of-
pocket expenditures from individual or household savings can expose
people who most need health care services to undue financial risk,
poverty, or destitution.

Cross-subsidies are the essence of health insurance. The effects of
cross-subsidization are shown in figure 1.2. Putting all participants' contributions into a single pool, and requiring contributions according to
capacity to pay, facilitates cross-subsidization and, depending on the size
of the resource pool, can significantly improve financial protection for

*Figure 1.2* Pooling Risks between High- and Low-Risk
Individuals

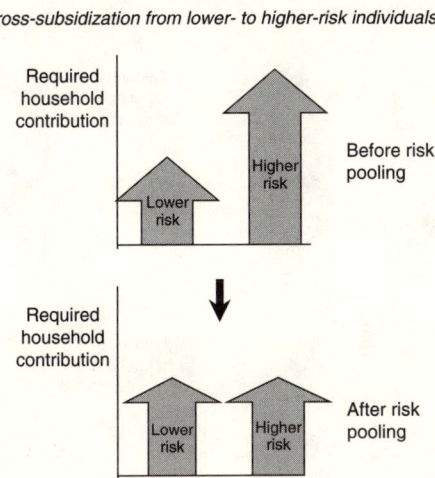

Source: Baeza et al. 2002, 24. Reproduced by permission.

every pool member. However, as discussed in chapter 6, reaching informal and unsalaried workers with this kind of contributory risk pooling poses significant problems because it gives households strong incentives for adverse selection and insurers strong incentives for risk-selection behavior.

Spreading risk through insurance schemes ensures equitable financial protection because it can result in subsidization of high-income, high-risk members by low-risk, low-income individuals. Furthermore, many impoverished people may be unable to pay anything at all, and contribution costs may perpetuate or deepen poverty among the borderline poor. For this reason, most health care financing policies attempt both to spread risk (like traditional insurance in any other sector) and to ensure the additional goal of equity in health financing. Thus, a prerequisite to financial protection is ensuring the availability of sufficient subsidies from high- to low-income households.

We distinguish the low-risk to high-risk subsidy (*risk subsidy*) from the subsidy that shifts costs from low- to high-income households

*Figure 1.3* How Risk-Pooling Systems Also Ensure Equity

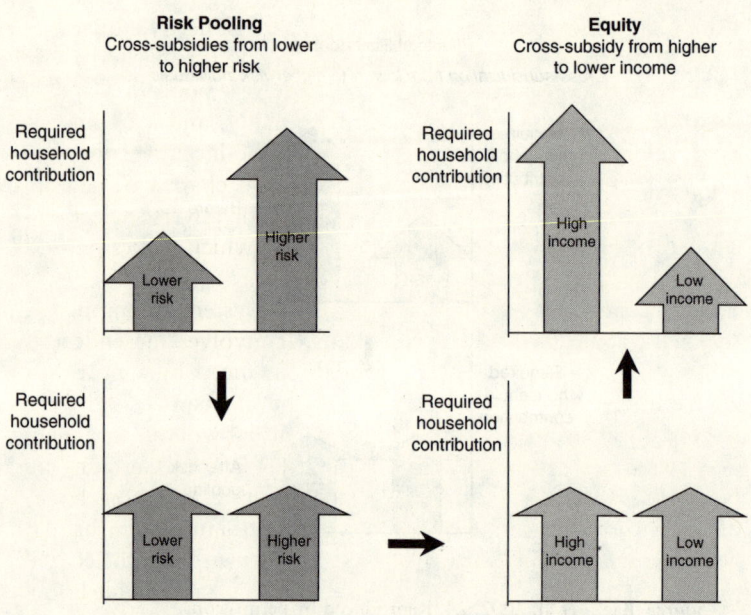

*Source:* Baeza et al. 2002, 25. Reproduced by permission.

*(equity subsidy)* as two separate objectives and effects of risk pooling in health. The two are illustrated in figure 1.3.

## Sources of Financing for an Equity Subsidy

There are at least three options for financing an equity subsidy: subsidies within a risk pool, subsidies across different risk pools, and public subsidies. Health care systems in LAC used one or a combination of these options. An in-depth analysis of each option is beyond the scope of this report, but a brief review of each illustrates the complexity of ensuring equity subsidy for the financial protection of everyone. It is also helpful in understanding the origins of some country health reforms analyzed in chapter 6.

Subsidies within the same risk-pooling arrangement are at the core of traditional social insurance (SI) systems financed through payroll taxes. The goal of collecting revenues through an income-related contribution (in contrast to a risk-related contribution) is to generate cross-subsidies from high- to low-income individuals and assist needy individuals. This system is optimal when salary contributions are feasible and a large part of the population participates in the same risk pool. In a system with multiple, competing insurers, high informality, and a fragmented risk pool, salary-related contributions increase the incentives for risk selection ("cherry-picking"). Also, as discussed in chapter 5, payroll taxes create incentives for nonparticipation and for adverse selection in the context of great and increasing informality, which makes participation in social security essentially voluntary.

The second option is to create a subsidy system among populations that participate in different risk pools. It involves the endowment of funds (often called "solidarity funds") financed by a portion of the contributions into each risk pool. This mechanism is used in systems with multiple insurers, usually covering formal workers and their families. Examples are found in the health systems of Germany and the Netherlands. In Latin America, Colombia and Argentina have introduced these equalization funds. The Colombian system has a single Solidarity Fund (FOSYGA) that attempts to ensure that the contributive modality (Régimen Contributivo) works as much as possible like a single risk pool, despite the multiple insurers in the system (Empresas Promotoras de Salud [EPS]). The success of this mechanism hinges on enforcing adequate compensation systems among different risk and income groups, risk adjustment, or both. Enacting this mechanism has proven technically and politically complex.

Finally, another option for financing the equity subsidy is public financing with funds generated via general taxation. This system is widely used in industrial countries to subsidize health care for some groups or for the entire population. It is also used in developing countries, though greatly restricted due to fiscal constraints, because large portions of the populations do not participate in the formal economy or they need subsidies to access health care services. It also occurs when social security organizations receive public subsidies either to cover their operational deficits (for example, Mexico's social security institutions for formal workers in the private sector and public sector workers) or to explicitly include informal workers and the poor in their schemes (for example, Chile's Fondo Nacional de Salud and Colombia's Régimen Subsidiado). In Colombia, this subsidy is also financed through one-percentage point of payroll tax contributions from participants in the Régimen Contributivo.

## Alternative Organizational Arrangements for Risk Pooling

Each society chooses a different way of pooling its people's financial risk to finance its health care system (figure 1.4). Most high income countries follow one of the two main models: the Bismarck model (Bismarck's Law on Health Insurance of 1883) or the Beveridge model (from the report on Social Insurance and Allied Services of 1942—the Beveridge Report). In most developing countries, multiple and fragmented forms of risk-pooling arrangements coexist.

In the Bismarck SI model, entitlement to benefits depends on an explicit contribution made by or on behalf of the covered person (for example, by breadwinners for their dependents, the state budget for defined categories of noncontributors). In a Beveridge type system, entitlement is typically a condition of citizenship or residence of the country. This difference is actually quite important. Specifically, under SI, entitlement is by definition not universal, and the issue of contribution by the self-employed nonpoor is central to the issue of coverage. Under a Beveridge-type arrangement, coverage is universal by definition, and tax collection from the self-employed nonpoor is not important in terms of entitlement for this group. However, the overall challenge of tax collection from this and other groups of the population is central to the extent

*Figure 1.4* Alternative Risk-Pooling Arrangements

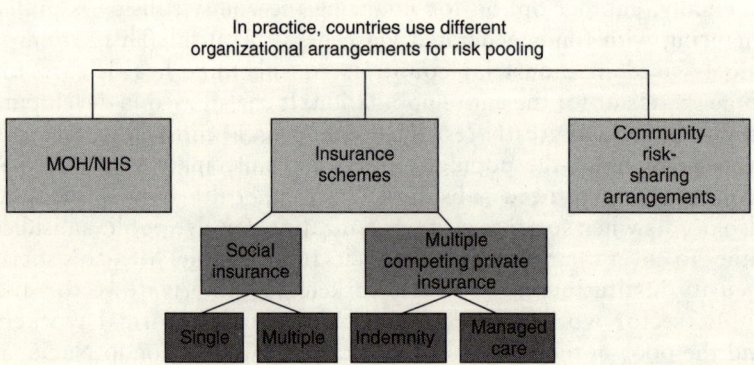

MOH=Ministry of health; NHS=national health service.
*Source:* Authors.

to which real effective financial protection can be sustained from only general tax revenues.

Each organizational arrangement for risk pooling has been historically linked to distinctive instruments for collecting revenue and buying health services. Whether a particular arrangement is truly a health insurance arrangement is often (erroneously) discussed in terms of the presence or absence of an earmarked, salary-related contribution collection mechanism (typically structured as a payroll tax). Instead, the real question is, "Does it spread risk?"

The most common organizational arrangements for risk pooling in the LAC region are: national health services or direct delivery through ministries of health; SI organizations; voluntary health insurance plans; and community-financing organizations or informal insurance schemes.

*NHSs or direct delivery through ministries of health* differ from other risk-pooling arrangements mainly in their revenue-collection mechanism. NHSs (derived from the Beveridge model) are financed mostly from general taxation. In contrast, the other three are normally based on earmarked contributions (either premiums or payroll taxes). Many NHSs also have large networks of public providers. In developing countries, this organizational arrangement usually provides services for the poor and workers in the informal sector. Many industrial countries have based their risk pooling in health completely on NHS or variations of this model (for example, France, New Zealand, Spain, Sweden, and the United Kingdom).

*SI organizations* (derived from the Bismarck model) can be either a single national organization or several organizations (competing or noncompeting). Usually they are funded via payroll taxes. The private sector may or may not participate in their management or ownership. Social insurance organizations (or "social security," as they are often called) traditionally provide services for workers in the formal sector and have their own networks of providers, buy services from other providers, or both. Many industrial countries rely on this model for their risk-pooling arrangements (for example, Germany, Netherlands, and U.S. Medicare).

*Voluntary health insurance* plans are usually risk-rated private insurance schemes financed by voluntary risk-based premiums. Only a few industrial countries rely mainly on this arrangement for risk pooling (for example, the United States for active workers in the formal labor market and Switzerland).

*Community financing organizations* or informal insurance schemes are organized to pool risks by members of a community, small groups of individuals, or provider organizations. These organizations are usually financed by voluntary contributions and often by variable amounts of public subsidization. Some forms of these organizations are also known as "micro-health-insurance" (Dror and Jacqier 1999). These organizations are much less prevalent in LAC than in other regions (for example, Africa and South Asia), and health financing specialists disagree about their effectiveness as risk-pooling arrangements (Baeza, Montenegro, and Núñez 2002.)

## Health Systems in Latin America and the Caribbean

Fragmentation is the most distinctive characteristic of LAC health systems. Within each system, different types of risk-pooling arrangements coexist, creating a complex set of incentives for households trying to cover their health care costs. These incentives not only shape how households decide to face potential financial losses from health shocks, but also influence life-style and economic decisions such as whether to work in the formal or informal sectors of the economy (see chapter 6).

The coexistence of risk-pooling structures varies from a predominance of the NHS arrangement in Honduras (about 90 percent of the population) (Fiedler 2004), to shared coverage by NHS and SI institutions in Mexico (Knaul et al. 2004), to a predominantly multiple SI arrangement in Argentina (57 percent of the population in 2002) (Maceira 2004), and a predominantly single SI in Costa Rica (90 percent of the population in 2000) (World Bank 2004a). The coexistence of risk-pooling structures often means the risk pool is broken up into many smaller pools, with no portability of benefits from one risk pool to another. Decentralization of service delivery to the states in Latin America's large federal countries, such as Argentina, Brazil, and Mexico (PAHO 2002), might exacerbate health care fragmentation if the federal-state interface does not work smoothly.

The last two decades have seen many health system reforms in the LAC region. Major reforms have been attempted by most countries in revenue collection, risk pooling (including health insurance), and purchasing, and by some countries in health service delivery. Several governments have succeeded with these reforms, while many others have not yet met their objectives. Some of the important trends and specific reforms are analyzed in chapter 6. Table 1.1 summarizes the current status of 16 LAC countries in terms of organization of the different health system functions.

*Table 1.1* General Health System Organizations Information in LAC, by Health Function, 2004

| Country | Stewardship | Financing | | Purchasing | Provision |
| | | Revenue[a] Collection | Risk Pooling | | |
| --- | --- | --- | --- | --- | --- |
| Argentina | Shared between provinces (significant decentralization) and federal level | 28% PRT<br>22% GT<br>31% OOP[b]<br>19% Other | Multiple:<br>Federal<br>Provincial<br>Social security organization (more than 300 Obras Sociales)<br>Private insurers | Provinces<br>Obras Sociales<br>Private insurers | Provincial health systems<br>Private provider |
| Barbados | Ministry of Health (MOH) | 0% PRT<br>68% GT<br>24% OOP<br>7% Other | Multiple:<br>MOH<br>Private insurers | Private insurers | Public providers<br>Private providers |
| Bolivia | Ministry of Health | 39% PRT<br>21% GT<br>33% OOP<br>8% Other | Multiple:<br>MOH<br>Social security<br>Private insurers | MOH<br>Private insurers | MOH<br>Social security<br>Private providers |

*(Table continues on the following page.)*

*Table 1.1* (continued)

| Country | Stewardship | Financing | | | Provision |
|---------|-------------|-----------|-----------|------------|-----------|
| | | Revenue[a] Collection | Risk Pooling | Purchasing | |
| Brazil | Federal Ministry of Health and states health ministries | 0% PRT 46% GT 35% OOP 19% Other | Multiple: Federal government States Municipalities (microregions) Private insurers | Federal government State governments Municipalities (microregions) Private insurers | Public providers Private providers |
| Chile | Ministry of Health directly and through the Superintendent of Health | 17% PRT 28% GT 27% OOP 28% Other | Multiple: FONASA Instituciones de Salud Previsional (ISAPREs) | FONASA ISAPREs Health districts | Public providers Private providers |
| Colombia | Ministry of Social Protection directly and through the Superintendent of Health | 49% PRT 34% GT 10% OOP 7% Other[b] | Multiple: Régimen Subsidiado Régimen Contributivo | EPSs ARSs | Public providers Private providers |
| | National Social Security Council | | MOH | Direcciones Seccionales de Salud (Departamentos y Distritos) | |

| Country | | | | | |
|---|---|---|---|---|---|
| Costa Rica | Ministry of Health | 54% PRT<br>11% GT<br>34% OOP | Single:<br>Social security (Caja Costarricense) | Social security (Caja Costarricense) | Mostly social security (Caja Costarricense) providers |
| Dominican Republic | Ministry of Health | 7% PRT<br>29% GT<br>56% OOP<br>8% Other[b] | Multiple:<br>Social security (Instituto Dominicano de Seguridad Social, IDSS)<br>Private health insurers | Private insurers<br>IDSS-selected services<br>MOH-selected services | MOH<br>Social security (IDSS)<br>Private for-profit providers |
| Ecuador | Ministry of Health | 13% PRT<br>23% GT<br>57% HH OOP<br>7% Other[b] | Multiple<br>Social security (Instituto Ecuatoriano de Seguridad Social, IESS)<br>Farmers' insurance (Seguro Social Campesino, SSC)<br>Private health insurers | MOH-selected services<br>Social security (IESS) for some services<br>Private insurers<br>Not-for-profit organizations | MOH<br>Social security (IESS)<br>Farmers' insurance (SSC)<br>Private not-for-profit providers<br>Private for-profit providers |
| Honduras | Ministry of Health | 9% PRT<br>42% GT<br>42% OOP<br>7% Other[b] | Multiple<br>Social security (Instituto Hondureño de Seguridad Social, IHSS)<br>Private health insurers | Social security (IHSS) for some services<br>Private insurers<br>Private firms | MOH<br>Social security (IHSS)<br>Private providers |

*(Table continues on the following page.)*

*Table 1.1* (continued)

| Country | Stewardship | Financing | | | Provision |
| | | Revenue[a] Collection | Risk Pooling | Purchasing | |
| --- | --- | --- | --- | --- | --- |
| Jamaica | Ministry of Health | 0% PRT 57% GT 26% OOP 16% Other[b] | Multiple: Private insurers | Private insurers | Public providers Private providers |
| Mexico | Shared between federal health secretary, social security (Instituto Mexicano de Seguridad Social, IMSS), Instituto de Seguridad y Servicios Sociales para los Trabajadores del Estado, (ISSSTE), and the states | 30% PRT 15% GT 52% OOP 3% Other[b] | Multiple: Federal health secretary State health systems Social security (IMSS) ISSSTE | State health systems Social security (IMSS and others) Private insurers | Social security providers (IMSS, ISSSTE) Private providers |
| Nicaragua | Ministry of Health | 14% PRT 35% GT 49% OOP 2% Other[b] | Multiple: Social security Private insurers | Private insurers | Public providers Private providers |

| Paraguay | Ministry of Health | 11% PRT 27% GT 55% OOP 7% Other [b] | Multiple: Social security Private insurers | Private insurers | Public providers Private providers |
|---|---|---|---|---|---|
| Trinidad and Tobago | Ministry of Health | 0% PRT 37% GT 54% OOP 9% Other [b] | Multiple: Private insurers | Private insurers | Public providers Private providers |
| Uruguay | Shared between the Ministry of Health and the Ministry of Finance | 16% PRT 13% GT 18% OOP 53% Other [b] | Multiple: State Health Service Administration (ASSE), Fondo Nacional de Recursos (FNR), Institutos de Asistencia Medica Colectiva (IAMC) | ASSE FNR IAMC | MOH providers Private providers |

PRT=payroll tax; GT=general taxation; OOP = out-of-pocket payment.

a. Represents a proxy estimated from health expenditures data.

b. This category includes household expenditures on private health insurance and other private risk-pooling mechanisms, expenditures of private companies, and private not-for- profit organizations.

*Sources:* PAHO 2002; WHO 2004; Baeza 2002.

# Note

1. The description of the way health systems function uses the terminology first presented in the *World Health Report 2000* by the World Health Organization (WHO 2000). The discussion of alternative risk-pooling arrangements and instruments for cross-subsidization is developed mostly from previous work by the STEP Program, run by the International Labor Organization (ILO) (Baeza, Crocco, Núñez, and Shaffer 2002).

# 2

# Health Shocks, Household Welfare, and the Risk of Poverty

HEALTH SHOCKS—adverse health events such as sickness, accidents, or normal life cycle events—not only sap the health of individuals but can also impoverish their households. In the wake of health shocks, households' consumption possibilities can be dramatically lowered. There are two potential sources of impoverishment: lost income due to reduced participation in the labor market and diminished productivity and household spending on health care and health insurance. Both causes are prevalent and require sound policy actions. However, because much has already been written on income losses from reduced labor market participation and productivity,[1] we focus mainly on the impoverishing impact of health expenditures resulting from inadequate financial protection.

The cost of treating a serious illness or injury can force individuals and households to cut nonmedical consumption and may curtail human capital accumulation for many years. Further, the cost of care can plunge households into poverty and perpetuate poverty for the already poor. For this reason, it is important for policy makers to maintain and improve the health status of the people they represent through cost-effective public health interventions. Equally important from a household perspective is to achieve this goal while ensuring that households are protected financially from falling into poverty.

From a public policy point of view, however, the relative importance of setting priorities for gains in health status or in financial protection varies significantly across countries. In poorer countries, with low life expectancy and tight resources, returns from assigning priority to health-enhancing interventions are much different from the returns from such a focus in middle-income countries that have already achieved long life expectancy. The evidence and discussion in these chapters are intended to encourage policy makers to consider, when setting their policy priorities, both the health status and the financial protection objectives of health systems. The decision on the relative importance of each objective will depend on the country context.

What is *financial protection* as a health system goal? A strict definition is just beginning to emerge among policy makers, specialists, and the academic community. On how much is too much for households to have to spend on health care, there is, as yet, little consensus. Experts do, however, agree that a household's spending on health should (at the very least) not cause a family's impoverishment or prevent a poor household from overcoming poverty. Nor should spending on health force a household to reduce consumption of other vital goods and services (such as food and education) and thus hinder the accumulation of human capital over the medium and longer term.

Before turning our discussion to financial protection measures, ways households seek to protect themselves from health shocks, alternative financing options, and policy implications, we focus in this chapter on empirical evidence of the impact of household health spending on welfare and the impoverishing impact of the cost of care. We show the magnitude of spending on health as a share of gross domestic product (GDP), how much of this spending households shoulder directly, and the extent of reported health-spending shocks relative to other income shocks. We then briefly review empirical work conducted in both developed and developing countries on the impact of health on productivity, income, and consumption and find that relatively little prior analytical work has been conducted to measure the impoverishing effect of health spending. We go on to present empirical evidence of the importance and impact of health spending shocks on household welfare, taken from six country case studies commissioned for this report. These country cases were selected to represent the diversity of health finance policies and institutions in the Latin America and the Caribbean (LAC) region today.

The chapter closes with a look at how LAC households are covered against the financial consequences of health shocks. Drawing on our case studies, we show the extent to which households are covered by formal health finance institutions—from national public health systems through which governments deliver care directly and which are typically financed out of general tax revenues, by quasi-public social insurance schemes, and by private health insurance plans.

## Country and Household Spending on Health

Around the world, health care costs are rising. Health care expenditures rose from 3 percent of world GDP in 1948 to 9.8 percent in 2001 (WHO 2000 and 2004). Though often imprecise and sometimes unreliable, country data on health expenditures are still useful to put LAC health expenditure in context with other parts of the world (table 2.1)[2]. With

*Table* 2.1 Composition of Health Financing in High-, Middle-, and Low-Income Countries (averages in 2001)

| Regions and Income Levels | Per Capita GDP (US$) | Per Capita Health Expenditure (US$) | Total Health Expenditures (%) GDP) | Public (% total public health expenditures) | Social Security (% total health expenditures) | Private Expenditures (% total health expenditures) | Out-of-Pocket Expenditures (% private health expenditures) | Private Prepaid Plan Expenditures (% private health expenditures) | External Expenditures (% total health expenditures) |
|---|---|---|---|---|---|---|---|---|---|
| East Asia and Pacific | 1,387 | 84 (46) | 5.6 | 59.3 | 11.1 | 40.7 | 83.4 | 3.5 | 11.9 |
| Eastern Europe and Central Asia | 2,053 | 132 (131) | 5.5 | 67.1 | 42.1 | 32.9 | 94.9 | 3.5 | 2.6 |
| Latin America and the Caribbean | 3,705 | 237 (264) | 6.4 | 58.2 | 28.5 | 43.8 | 81.5 | 13.7 | 4.0 |
| Middle East and North Africa | 2,834 | 102 (82) | 5.6 | 52.7 | 15.6 | 47.3 | 79.1 | 8.1 | 3.1 |
| South Asia | 737 | 38 (21) | 4.6 | 49.0 | 6.2 | 51 | 97.7 | 0.2 | 9.9 |
| Sub-Saharan Africa | 868 | 42 (29) | 4.5 | 54.0 | 1.0 | 46 | 83.3 | 6.9 | 21.7 |
| High-income countries | 21,198 | 1,527 (2,860) | 7.7 | 70.1 | 33.1 | 29.9 | 74.0 | 16.2 | 0.1 |
| Middle-income countries | 3,026 | 176 (106) | 5.8 | 61.7 | 28.2 | 38.3 | 86.4 | 8.9 | 3.4 |
| Low-income countries | 576 | 25 (19) | 4.7 | 51.7 | 2.2 | 48.3 | 84.4 | 4.0 | 20.0 |

*Note:* All figures are weighted by country; per capita health expenditures include population-weighted averages in parentheses.
*Source:* Schieber et al. 2006.

total health expenditures accounting for 6.4 percent of GDP, LAC is the highest expending region in the world. Only high-income countries spend more on average as a percentage of GDP than LAC. However, LAC ranks third in terms of total public expenditures on health as a percentage of total health expenditures (56.2 percent), after Asia and Pacific and Eastern Europe and Central Asia. This is not surprising, considering the region's poor tax performance (chapter 5)—better only than in Sub-Saharan Africa and South Asia.

Diverse country contexts underlie regional averages, and the mixed picture in LAC reflects the region's diversity. As shown in figure 2.1, most LAC countries spend less than expected for their GDP per capita in terms of total fiscal expenditures as a proportion of total health expenditures. Notable exceptions are Colombia, Costa Rica, and Bolivia.

Because public expenditures on health (fiscal and other) are low, private health expenditures are high in most LAC countries. This would not necessarily be problematic if those private expenditures reflected high demand for private contributory health insurance, but it does not in most LAC countries. By far, most private health expenditures in the

*Figure 2.1* Total Fiscal Expenditures on Health as a
Percentage of Total National Health
Expenditures and GDP per Capita (in PPP)

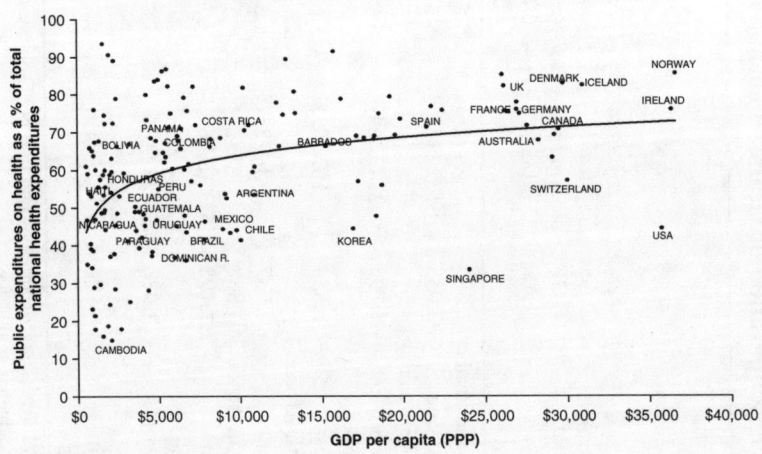

*Sources:* WHO 2004 and UNDP 2004.

*Figure 2.2* Total Out-of-Pocket Health Care Expenditures
as a Percentage of Total National Health
Expenditures and GDP per Capita (in PPP)

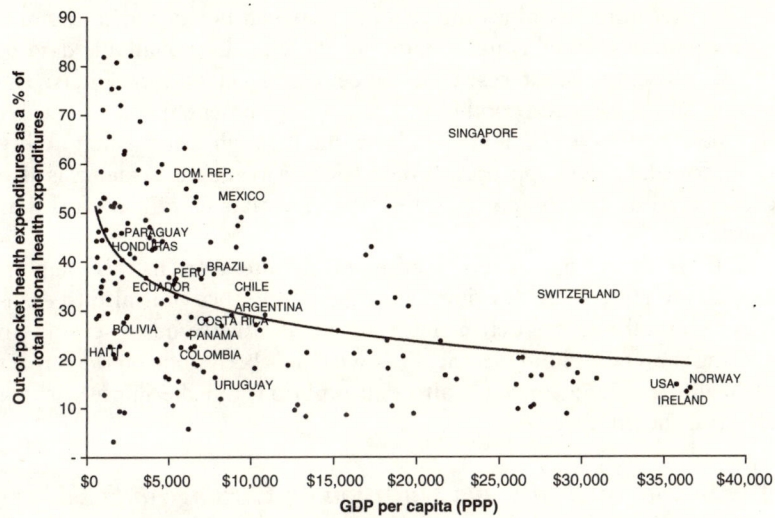

*Sources:* WHO 2004 and UNDP 2004.

region come directly out of pocket the moment public or private health services are sought. Figure 2.2 shows that most LAC countries spend a higher-than-expected proportion of out-of-pocket (nonpooled) expenditures in relation to their GDP per capita. Notable exceptions are Uruguay and Colombia.

In LAC, the private share of health spending averages 45 percent. Although this share is much lower in some Caribbean countries (at around 20 percent), the regional average is much higher than in Europe and the Organisation for Economic Co-operation and Development (OECD) countries, where private spending can be as low as 9 percent (Czech Republic), and as high as 37 percent (Netherlands), and 56 percent (United States).

The most relevant available spending indicator of the impact of health spending on individual and household consumption and welfare is the share of private out-of-pocket spending on health by households in contrast to the share they put into risk-pooling arrangements (see chapter 5).

## Evidence of the Impact of Health
## on Household Income

Most of the empirical work linking individual and household welfare to health covers the impact of health on productivity and earnings.[3] Much of this literature examines the relation between health indicators and earnings in developed countries, due to the wealth of available data in these countries. Most research concentrates on two channels: the impact of nutrition and good health on earnings potential and the impact of illness and injury on household income through lost earning ability or forgone labor. As appropriate data become available, evidence is also growing from developing countries where similar empirical work has been done.

But, as shown in the review of empirical literature in this chapter, despite the large body of evidence on the importance of health to earnings potential and the detrimental impact of adverse health events on earnings and household income, little work has been done on the impact of health spending on nonhealth consumption and the impoverishing effects of health care costs.

### The Impact of Health and Nutrition on Earning Ability

Several researchers have found an empirical link between health and nutrition in infancy and childhood and earning outcomes later in life. In an analysis of the impact of health on the future earning capacity of individuals in LAC, Savedoff and Schultz (2000) find that healthier people (as measured by different health status variables) receive higher wages.[4] Knaul (1999), focusing on Mexico, uses age at menarche (defined as the onset of the first menstrual cycle) as a health indicator of the long-term (secular) effects of investments in childhood nutrition and other early childhood factors that affect adult health. Knaul concludes that a one-year decrease in the reported age at menarche is associated with an increase of 23 percent to 26 percent in wages.

Ribero and Nuñez (1999), analyzing public and private investments in health in Colombia, used instrumental variables to identify the magnitude of labor market returns from good health status. The authors analyzed two indicators of health: disability and number of days disabled. The authors found that each additional day of disability decreased earnings between 13 percent and 33 percent. In contrast, each additional centimeter of stature increased future earnings by 7 or 8 percent. Comparing rural and urban residents, the authors discovered that estimations of health production indicate that investments in nutrition are critically important to individuals' future returns in the labor market.

The relation between health and income has also been analyzed from the perspective of nutrition among working-age individuals. Economic theories incorporating this association—known as the "efficiency wage" hypothesis—have been argued in the literature since the 1950s. Although the connection seems intuitively logical, complex measurement issues limit the availability of supporting evidence.[5] Advances in household surveys have given researchers access to new data that allow them to better model and analyze these theories. The association between healthy nutritional status and higher labor productivity is particularly relevant for developing countries in which much of the economy and the population depend directly or indirectly on agricultural activities that require intensive physical labor.

Deolalikar (1988) examines nutrition and labor productivity in the agricultural sector in rural South India. The author, using weight-for-height as the anthropometric measurement for nutritional status, concludes that nutritional status plays a critical role in determining labor productivity in agriculture. Ferrando, Hernández, and Savedoff (1999), using self-reported illness and days of illness, show that health status determinants affect individual productivity as measured by hourly income. The authors show that poor health can reduce productivity by as much as 58 percent and that better health status is associated with higher hourly income.

## Income Losses from Forgone Work due to Sickness or Injury

Ill health and accidents can cause households to lose income through several channels. Households face the cost of productive time lost due to sickness of working members, as well as opportunity costs due to days spent taking care of ill family members. Income lost due to sickness has been extensively studied in developed countries. In the United States, several studies on common conditions have shown a strong connection between sickness and lower income. Stewart et al. (2003) examine losses in productive time due to common pain conditions in the workforce. According to the results, 13 percent of the total workforce reported a loss in productive time due to conditions that caused some of the most common forms of pain—headaches, back pain, arthritis pain, and pain due to other musculoskeletal conditions.[6]

Blanc et al. (2001) conducted a study of asthma and rhinitis in northern California. Participation in the adult labor force since the onset of this condition was lower among those with asthma than among those with rhinitis alone. Among those still employed, decreased job effectiveness was more frequently reported by the rhinitis sufferers than by the asthmatics. Lost work attributable to these conditions was common in both groups: more than 20 percent reported one or more full or partial workdays lost in the four weeks prior to being interviewed.

Boden and Galizzi (1999) use individual data to estimate earnings lost from all reported workplace injuries and illnesses in the United States. The authors found that lost-time injuries and illness produce both physical effects, caused by reduced work capacity, and labor-market effects, caused by long-term work absence while recovering. The labor-market impact may be caused by loss of seniority, by a forced switch from a union job to a nonunion job, by stigma associated with on-job injuries, or by valuable labor market experience forgone due to injury. According to the research, the average value of losses projected 10 years beyond the observed period is equivalent to more than $8,000 per injury. Women were found to lose a greater proportion of their preinjury earnings than men.

Several studies focus on diseases that affect large groups of the population. Cisternas et al. (2003), examining the direct and indirect costs of adult asthma, find that work loss is an important part of indirect costs. Productive time lost due to asthmatic conditions among adults was estimated at 61 percent of total indirect costs, even though only 5 percent was related to absenteeism.

In a recent study on the dynamics of poverty and social exclusion in Great Britain, Gordon (2002) shows that severe ill health is a major cause of poverty through lost income. The author points to a rapid decline in income due to sickness as the primary culprit. Another possible connection inferred from this study is that disabling conditions that require early retirement can lead to rapid reduction in incomes.

Bodger (2002) focuses on chronic disease in the United Kingdom and shows that high direct and indirect costs are associated with chronic disease. Long periods of absenteeism and early disability can lower patients' earnings, even if most patients (90 percent) remain in the workforce and have a normal life expectancy. A study conducted in Germany by Lederer, Weltle, and Weber (2001) confirms that chronic conditions that force civil servants into sharp declines in productivity and increases in absenteeism lead them to lose their sources of income and apply for early retirement.

Cortez (1999) focuses on measuring the effect of health on the hourly wage of adult men and women in rural and urban Peru. This research indicates that good health is an asset to productivity as measured by wages. The authors show that the rate of illness and number of days of illness reported in national surveys is negatively related to individual wages and household income. The author estimates that one less day of reported illness in a month increases the wages of urban and rural women by 3.4 percent and 6.2 percent, respectively. For men, the increase was higher—4.7 percent and 14.2 percent, respectively, in urban and rural areas.

Murrugarra and Valdivia (1999) discuss the returns on health for Peruvian urban adults by gender, age, and across wage distribution by estimating the earnings impact of health status. Health status (measured by days of reported illness) was found to have a strong and positive impact on wages, especially for men. The effects of illness are greatest on the lowest paid workers, whose hourly wages are reduced by 3.8 percent for each sick day. Results also suggest that the impact on wages is stronger for jobs in which productivity is closely tied to health.

Parker (1999) examines earnings in the labor market using several health status determinants among the elderly in Mexico. This is one of the first studies to explore the relation between health and wages among the elderly in a developing country. Parker demonstrates that poor health lowers the hourly earnings of elderly males by 58 percent.[7]

Jayawardene (1993), using data from India, breaks down the cost of malaria between its effects on the household head and other household members through direct and indirect costs. Indirect costs include delay of farming activities, loss of time and workdays, indebtedness resulting from expenditure, and lost income. The greatest loss was incurred from the illness of the household head, equivalent to an average of 8.36 wage days over a 10-month period. Added to this was the indirect cost for other family members: an average of 5.3 days, yielding a total average of 13.7 days lost when the household head was ill. The loss of a day's work because of malaria meant the loss of a day's wages, and the average wage was approximately 40 rupees per day.[8]

Mills (1994) reports the results of an investigation into the economic consequences of malaria for households in Nepal. According to the study results, most households cope with the reduced labor supply during a malaria episode without great difficulty by drawing largely on other adult family members.

De Codes, Baker, and Schumann (1988) develop and use country examples to highlight the indirect cost of illness based on the economic value of human life and on other consequences for households, including productivity losses that can reduce family income. The cost of injuries was found to be more than five times greater than any specific disease, greater than the whole group of ill-defined conditions, and only slightly smaller than the category of all other diseases combined due to indirect costs.

Though less prevalent, several studies show the adverse effect of sickness on household income when income earners miss work to care for sick family members. Principi et al. (2003) examine the socioeconomic impact of influenza on healthy children and their families in Italy. The authors find that parents of children with influenza missed more work than the parents of healthy children because they were needed at home to care for sick children. The loss of both paternal and maternal workdays was much higher in unvaccinated households than in vaccinated households.

Smith et al. (2002) conducted a study of employment barriers among welfare recipients and applicants with chronically ill children in the United States. The study was conducted in San Antonio, Texas, on 504 predominantly low-income English- or Spanish-speaking parents or primary caretakers of children aged 2 to 12 years with one of seven chronic illnesses. In their study, the authors found that current and former welfare recipients and welfare applicants were more likely than those with no contact with the welfare system to report that their children's illness adversely affected their employment.

## Policy Mechanisms to Address Household Losses of Income Due to Health Shocks

All industrial countries have public policies to compensate for income loss resulting from health shocks. Most countries in the LAC region have introduced many of these mechanisms for formal workers as part of social security benefits. Table 2.2 summarizes the most common mechanisms in place in the region.

*Table 2.2* Most Frequent Mechanisms to Compensate for Income Loss Resulting from Health Shocks in Latin America and the Caribbean

| Policy | Benefits | Duration of Benefits |
|---|---|---|
| Medical (sick) leave | Continuation of salary while absent for medical reasons | Temporary |
| Maternity leave | Continuation of salary while parent absent for childbirth | Temporary |
| Workers' accident insurance | May cover medical expenditures as well as workers' income while sick | Temporary |
| Maternal leave due to sickness of dependant children | Continuation of salary while absent due to sickness of dependent children | Temporary |
| Workers' disability insurance | Protection against income loss due to temporary or permanent disability payable either as lump sum or annuity | Temporary or Permanent |
| Early retirement due to disability | Accelerated pension benefit that may be paid in case of permanent disability | Permanent |
| Life insurance | Protection against income loss due to death of income earner (lump sum or annuity) | Permanent |
| Spousal and dependent benefits | Annuity payable upon death of income earner | Permanent |

*Source:* Authors' analysis.

Medical (sick) and maternity leave are among the most common benefits to protect workers from income loss due to a health shock. The economic impact of medical leave on firms' costs has been the focus of numerous analyses in both developed and developing countries because workers' use of these benefits has increased (Gunderson and Hyatt 2000; Neuhauser and Raphael 2004). Concern is growing that medical leave is becoming a substitute for ineffective or nonexistent unemployment insurance (Tokman, Rodríguez, and Larraín 2004).

Usually, in the private sector, medical leave for short periods of time (days to weeks) is planned as part of workers' total number of days' absent, together with vacations. For longer medical leave, private insurance (accident or disability insurance), social security, or other arrangements may protect against income loss.

Professional or work-related accident insurance is usually designed to provide protection against health care related expenditures due to accidents directly related to work. However, some such insurance may provide, as an additional benefit, income-loss protection for health shocks related to occupational hazards or injuries. Worker disability insurance, on the other hand, is designed to protect against income loss related to disabilities that prevent individuals from working for longer periods of time than those covered by medical leave or accident insurance.

Legal provisions that protect a worker's possibility of returning to a job after a long absence due to a medical condition also help protect households from income-loss shocks. Depending on each country's regulatory and legal framework, accident and disability insurance are managed by the private sector, by social security institutions, or by both.

Individuals prevented from working by certain types of permanent disabilities may be offered early retirement if they have contributed to their pension system for a minimum number of years. Early retirement is thus another income-protection alternative in case of health shocks.

Life insurance and spousal and dependent benefits protect households against permanent income loss due to the death of income earners. Life insurance is usually paid as a lump sum, particularly by private insurers. Sometimes insurance is designed to pay survivors an annuity to furnish an income stream over longer periods. Spousal and dependent income benefits to protect survivors are common provisions of social security systems. For children, such benefits usually stop at the age of legal majority, although in some cases this benefit is extended longer (for example, in Chile the Armed Forces system extends this benefit for life to unmarried daughters).

## Cost of Health Care and Its Impact on Consumption

There are at least two approaches to analyzing consumption variations due to changes in health status of household members. The first type studies how sickness affects consumption via income losses or the reduction of income-generating activities. The second type analyzes how health care expenditures affect the consumption of other nonhealth care goods and services.

Gertler and Gruber (2002) examine whether households can cope with severe ill-health shocks without cutting nonmedical consumption. The authors use data from a panel survey from Indonesia evaluating changes in the health status of the household head as well as other members of the family over a two-year period. According to the results, changes (from highest to lowest score) in a constructed indicator for activities of daily living (ADL) are associated with a reduction of roughly 20 percent in per capita consumption. Families can maintain their normal consumption of nonmedical goods and services as long as the illness does not affect the physical functioning of the household head. The more severe the illness of the household head, the more difficult it is to ensure prehealth shock consumption for the family.

Sauerborn et al. (1995) examine the coping strategies of rural households from Burkina Faso and suggest that illness-caused labor losses can reduce poor households' income. This study also found that health care related expenditures that were outside the scope of the usual household budget depleted or used up household savings and other assets.

Mock et al. (2003) find that in Ghana treatment costs were higher in urban than in rural areas. Although injuries in the urban area had a more severe primary effect, the ultimate effect on rural households appeared more severe. A greater percentage of rural households reported that treatment costs forced them to reduce food consumption than did urban households.

Finally, Wagstaff and Pradhan (2003) analyze the impact of out-of-pocket health expenditures on household consumption patterns in Vietnam. The authors use data from a panel survey that permit comparison of households before and after the introduction of Vietnam's health insurance system in 1993. The authors found that individuals covered by health insurance enjoyed 12 percent higher nonmedical consumption than those without coverage.

Table 2.3 presents a summary of the literature reviewed in this section (discussed in depth in Montenegro and Nazerali 2004). The literature from both developed and developing countries presents ample evidence of the links between health events and household income and

Table 2.3 Evidence Linking Health and Consumption through Lower Labor Supply and Lost Earnings

| Year | Author | Country | N | Unit of Analysis | Type of Study Quantitative | Type of Study Qualitative | Independent Variable of Interest | Dependent Variable |
|------|--------|---------|---|------------------|-------------|-------------|----------------------------------|--------------------|
| 2002 | Babu | India | 186 | Individuals | X | | Chronic lymphatic filariasis | Working hours/day |
| 2001 | Blanc | USA | 300 | Individuals | X | | Asthma and rhinitis | Work days lost |
| 1999 | Boden and Galizzi | USA | 70,377 | Individuals | X | | Workplace injuries | Annualized average earning losses |
| 2002 | Bodger | Sweden | N/A | Individuals | X | | Crohn's Disease | Early retirement |
| 2002 | Bodger | Sweden | N/A | Individuals | X | | Crohn's Disease | Future person yrs. lost before old-age pension |
| 2002 | Bodger | Sweden | N/A | Individuals | X | | Crohn's Disease | Sickness leave |
| 2003 | Cisternas | USA | 401 | Individuals | X | | Adult asthma | Total annual costs due to lost productivity |

(Table continues on the following page.)

*Table 2.3* (continued)

| Year | Author | Country | N | Unit of Analysis | Type of Study | | Independent Variable of Interest | Dependent Variable |
|------|--------|---------|---|------------------|---------------|---|----------------------------------|--------------------|
| | | | | | Quanti-tative | Quali-tative | | |
| 1999 | Cortez | Peru | 11,506 | Individuals | X | | Decrease in days of illness (women) | Wages |
| 1999 | Cortez | Peru | 18,766 | Individuals | X | | Decrease in days of illness (men) | Wages |
| 1988 | deCodes | Brazil | 872 | Households | | X | Injury | Indirect costs (including income) |
| 1988 | Deolaikar | South India | 240 | Households | X | | Weight for height (as a measure of health status) | Direction of the effect on wages |
| 2002 | Gordon | UK | N/A | N/A | | X | Sickness | Income lost |
| 2002 | Gordon | UK | N/A | N/A | | X | Severe ill health | Poverty |
| 1993 | Jaya-wardene | Sri Lanka | 124 | Households | X | | Head of household with malaria | Wage days lost |

| 1999 | Knaul | Mexico | 3,155 | Individuals | X | Decline of one year in age at menarche | Wages |
| 2001 | Lederer | Germany | 9,348 | Individuals | X | Mental illness | Income lost |
| 1994 | Mills | Nepal | 616 | Individuals | X | Episode of malaria | Mean days disabled per worker ill |
| 2003 | Mock | Ghana | 21,105 | Individuals | X | Days of illness | Disability days (not worked) |
| 1999 | Murrugarra and Valdivia | Peru | 1,144 | Individuals | X | Days of illness | Wages |
| 1999 | Ribero and Nuñez | Colombia | 18,866 | Households | X | Days of disability | Earnings |
| 1999 | Ribero and Nuñez | Colombia | 18,866 | Households | X | Increase in height | Earnings higher earnings |
| 1996 | Sauerborn | Burkina Faso | 566 | Households | X | Seasonal variation of household's time cost due to work incapacity | Illness during rainy season |

*(Table continues on the following page.)*

*Table 2.3* (continued)

| Year | Author | Country | N | Unit of Analysis | Type of Study | | Independent Variable of Interest | Dependent Variable |
|------|--------|---------|---|------------------|---------------|---|----------------------------------|--------------------|
| | | | | | *Quanti-tative* | *Quali-tative* | | |
| 1995 | Sauerborn | Burkina Faso | 4,820 | Households | | X | | Reduction in savings and assets |
| 1995 | Sauerborn | Burkina Faso | 566 | Households | | X | | Work days lost |
| 1995 | Sauerborn | Burkina Faso | 4,820 | Individuals | | X | | Labor loss |
| 2002 | Smith | USA | 504 | Individuals | | X | | Parents employment |
| 2003 | Stewart | USA | 28,902 | Individuals | X | | Reports a child with chronic illness Reports an episode of any chronic pain condition in past 2 weeks | Productive hours lost |

*Source:* Montenegro and Nazerali 2004.

consumption. However, there is relatively little evidence on the impact of health care costs on nonmedical consumption and on the impoverishing impact of these health costs.

This gap in the literature raises concern because financial losses from the cost of care can be as large or larger than income losses during acute health shocks or over long periods of costly treatment of chronic diseases. In the next section, we present empirical evidence of the magnitude of household spending on health care and on the risk of poverty presented by these costs.

## The Impact of Health Spending Shocks on Household Welfare in Six Latin American and Caribbean Countries

Earlier in this chapter, we presented comparative data compiled by the World Health Organization on health spending in several LAC countries and compared these indicators with similar data from the European Union and some of the wealthy OECD countries. A simple observation drawn from this comparison is that, although LAC countries spend less as a share of GDP on health, the portion of private spending is higher and private out-of-pocket spending by households is much higher.

### Adverse Health Events and Shocks to Household Income

Although household out-of-pocket spending accounts for 85 percent of private health expenditure in the LAC region, the high proportion of out-of-pocket spending does not in itself reflect lower welfare or greater vulnerability. Figure 2.3 presents the distribution of reported income losses from various adverse events, including job loss, political turmoil, death, disability, and the treatment of sickness. The data are taken from two surveys (*Encuesta de Prevision de Riesgos Sociales* [PRIESO] surveys) conducted in Chile and Peru that were designed to capture information on household risk management and strategies for coping with income shocks.[9] Respondents were allowed to report as many different income shocks as they wished, and the figures show a frequency distribution of responses in each category of shock (as a percentage of total responses). Although the questions posed did not ask specifically about health expenditures (as opposed to, for example, lost income due to illness), it is likely that respondents were referring to excessive expenditures when they reported "sickness costly to treat."

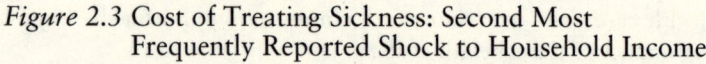

*Figure 2.3* Cost of Treating Sickness: Second Most
            Frequently Reported Shock to Household Income

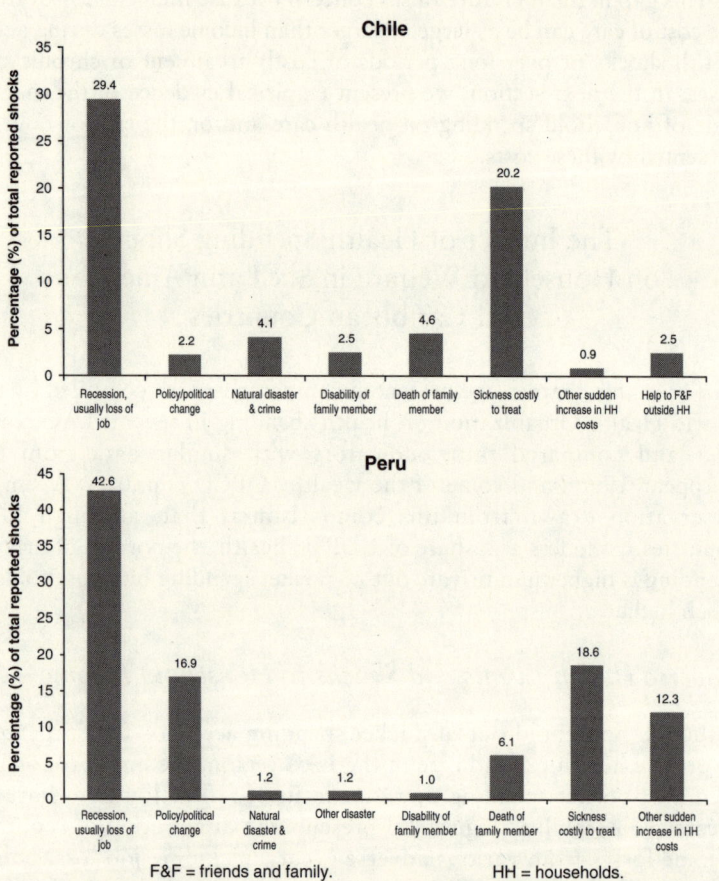

F&F = friends and family.                    HH = households.

*Note:* Both figures represent responses to the survey question "In the past
three years, has your household experienced an event that has caused a
significant loss in income?"

*Sorucs:* Chile, Packard 2005; Peru, authors using data from the Peru
PRIESO survey of 2002.

In the PRIESO surveys, the most frequently reported shock to
income was associated with economic recessions. When probed,
respondents mentioned job losses and extended unemployment or a
downturn in business if they were self-employed. Particularly striking in

the distribution from both surveys is that "sickness costly to treat" is the second most frequently reported shock. Often, respondents also reported "disability of a family member" and "death of a family member"—both of which could also be construed as adverse health events. If those responses were added in, health shocks closely rival earnings losses from unemployment as the most prevalent income shock. The responses on disability and death of household members do not, however, reveal whether the shock arose primarily from loss of income due to missed days of work, the cost of treatment, or some combination of both. However, the survey data from Chile and Peru presented in figure 2.3 clearly indicate that households perceive the direct costs that arise from adverse health events as posing significant constraints on their resources and that these events are important among reported shocks to household welfare.

Motivated by the increasing concern in health system policy analysis about the impoverishing consequences of health shocks (WHO 2000; Baeza et al. 2002; Wagstaff and Pradhan 2003) and by the suggestive household responses from the PRIESO surveys, we commissioned specific analyses of health shocks and household income and consumption in six LAC countries. The six country cases—Argentina, Chile, Colombia, Ecuador, Honduras, and Mexico—were selected to reflect both the diversity of the region and their different approaches to health finance (examined in later chapters). As per methodological comparability purposes, only data from Argentina, Chile, Colombia, and Ecuador are presented in this chapter, except regarding out-of-pocket expenditures for a standardized package of services, for which data from Mexico is presented (figure 2.4).

Readers are advised to interpret the findings of our country case studies with caution. The absence of a culture of household-centered analysis and evaluation of health system performance in LAC, particularly on financial protection, has meant a dearth of data for analysis of household financial protection against a health shock. The lack of good household data on health expenditure forces researchers to marshal sophisticated measurement techniques and sometimes make strong assumptions. For these reasons, the results presented in this chapter on the impoverishing effects of health shocks constitute preliminary evidence intended mostly to increase awareness among policy makers and to introduce an incentive for improved data collection and further analysis of this topic.

In the rest of this chapter, we present indicators of household out-of-pocket spending, measures of impoverishing spending, and the incidence of poverty after health shocks. The chapter closes with a look at the extent of coverage of public, quasi-public, and private health finance organizations designed to help households cover their health costs.

*Distribution of Household Expenditure and Impoverishing*
*Out-of-Pocket Spending on Health*

Figure 2.4 shows side-by-side comparisons of monthly household out-of-pocket health care expenditure (as a percentage of total household monthly income or consumption, depending on the data available in each country). The data from four country cases are presented by quintile of total household income, where quintile 1 represents the poorest 20 percent of households and quintile 5 the wealthiest 20 percent.

The poorest quintile spends a larger proportion of income on out-of-pocket health costs than the richest quintile. This higher proportion not only implies less disposable income for other consumption but, for the poor, can also erect an imposing barrier to necessary health services because the better-off show a larger price elasticity for health services than the nonpoor (Gertler and Van der Gaag 1988).

That demand for and spending on health care rises with income is well documented—as people become better-off, they can afford and actually seek better quality care and increasingly elective and costly procedures. Figure 2.4 also includes indicators of standardized spending out-of-pocket on a uniform package of health services and treatment. The figure shows actual reported spending out-of-pocket beside a measure of expenditure that adjusts actual reported spending by the inpatient use rate of households in the third income quintile. This adjustment, although methodologically different, follows the rationale for adjusting actual utilization to a standard utilization suggested by Pradhan and Prescott (2002). Without this adjustment, we would simply observe the differential of health care consumption between the lowest and the richest quintiles. Low out-of-pocket spending in households from lower income quintiles can merely reflect low utilization of services. If low-income households do not use services, they will not pay as much out-of-pocket, and the spending reported in most household surveys will show misleadingly low out-of-pocket health expenditure as a percentage of all expenditures. Standardizing the package to the same level of utilization is essential to judge the impact of out-of-pocket spending on total expenditures. This means comparing out-of-pocket spending in a hypothetical scenario where all households demand the same package of services, in this case the level of inpatient care observed in the particular country among households in the third quintile.

This adjustment is not without methodological problems—in our adjustment, the strong assumption that the need for health services among the lowest income quintile would be the same as in the third quintile. In

*Figure 2.4* Out-of-Pocket Health Spending on Health Services and Projected Out-of-Pocket Health Expenditures on a Standarized Package of Services

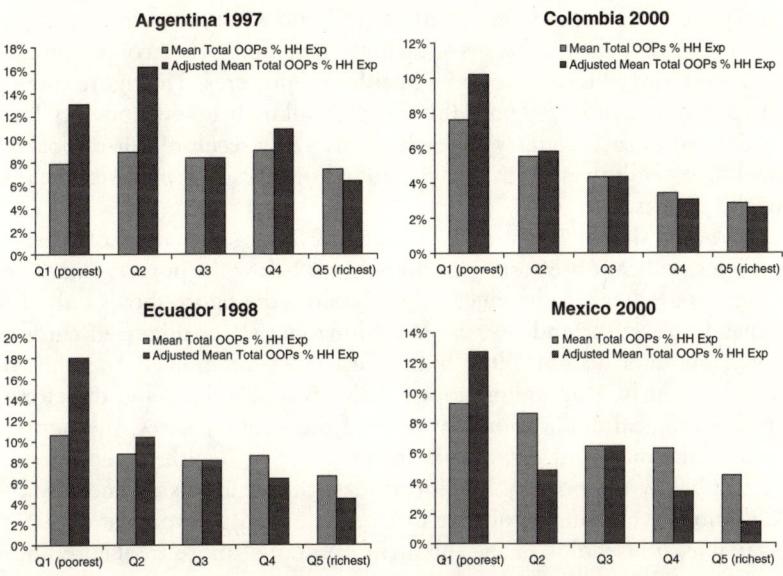

*Note:* Total out-of-pocket health spending as percentage of total household income or consumption by income quintile, actual and adjusted by inpatient use rate.OOP = out-of-pocket. HH = households.

*Sources:* Argentina, Maceira (2004); Colombia, Bitran et al. (2004); Ecuador, Montenegro (2004); and Mexico, Knaul et al. (2004).

practice, evidence suggests that the poor, with their greater incidence of health events, need the services more than the better-off. This assumption implies an underestimation of out-of-pocket expenditures even after the adjustment. However, since a standard package of services does not exist in most countries (or did not until recently), the adjustment allows us to calibrate household expenditure on health care, controlling for lack of demand for necessary services.

Although the actual reported spending on health presented by income quintile shows a mixed pattern—falling with income in some cases and rising in others—it is immediately apparent that out-of-pocket health expenditures on the standard package of services are highest among households in the lower income distribution groups.

## Impoverishing Out-of-Pocket Expenditure on Health

As mentioned at the beginning of this chapter, health specialists do not yet agree what constitutes excessive spending on health care. However, there is preliminary agreement that household spending on health should be considered excessive or catastrophic if it plunges households into poverty or impairs their capacity to build and sustain human capital. Figure 2.5 shows the share of households in each income quintile that are plunged into poverty by health expenditures. The figure shows the percentage of *newly poor* (households falling below the poverty line as defined in each country) in each quintile as a result of out-of-pocket health expenditures. Most newly poor households report significant health shocks.

The data shown in figures 2.5, 2.6, and 2.7 suggest that health shocks push a significant proportion of households below the poverty line. The numbers are likely to be much larger because the figure shows only the expenditure effect and not the loss-of-income effect discussed earlier. Available data do not allow both effects to be combined and shown simultaneously. Due to limitations in the available data, and therefore, methodological applications in most of the country cases, the figures represent household disposable income, net of health expenditures, falling below the poverty line for at least three months. In the case of Colombia, where inpatient data differentiated from outpatient data are available, households facing inpatient events fall more frequently into poverty and remain in poverty for up to a year.

Besides making it impossible to combine the expenditures and the income-loss effects, the available data present another major shortcoming: they preclude examination of the impact of shocks on consumption. A further limitation is that researchers cannot examine the long-term effects of health shock–triggered reductions in consumption on human capital formation. Nevertheless, our intention is to call attention to the poverty-generating effects of health shocks and suggest directions for further research. Only analysis using still-rare panel surveys of household consumption, health shocks, and proxies for human capital formation in the LAC region would generate more definitive findings to motivate policy. Gathering these data and exploring this dimension are critical to answering the questions that motivate this report.

Why do households fall into poverty? What mechanisms are available to protect them from impoverishment as a result of health shocks? What is failing or missing in LAC health systems that prevents them from being effective in preventing poverty? The remaining chapters of this report attempt to answer these questions from existing evidence.

*Figure 2.5* Out-of-Pocket Health Expenditures Due to Health Shocks Produce a Significant Number of Newly Poor

Argentina 1997: Percentage of individuals who become newly poor due to health shock by household consumption quintile

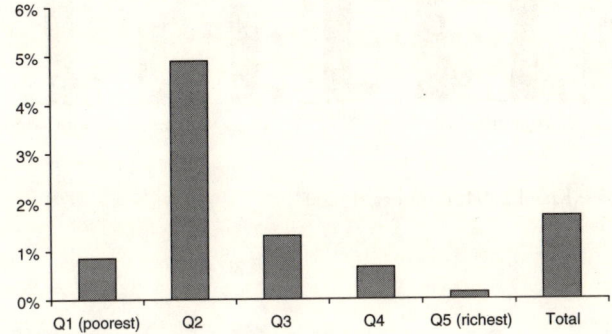

*Source:* Maceira 2004.

Chile 2000: Percentage of individuals who become newly poor due to a health shock by household consumption quintile

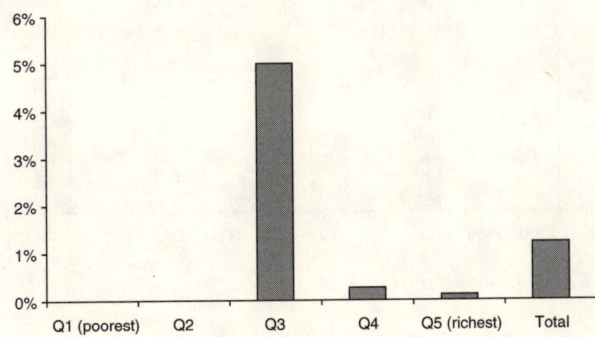

*Source:* Bitran et al. 2004.

*(Figure continues on the following page.)*

## *Figure 2.5* (continued)

Colombia 2003: Percentage of individuals who experience catastrophic out-of-pocket expenditure by household consumption quintile

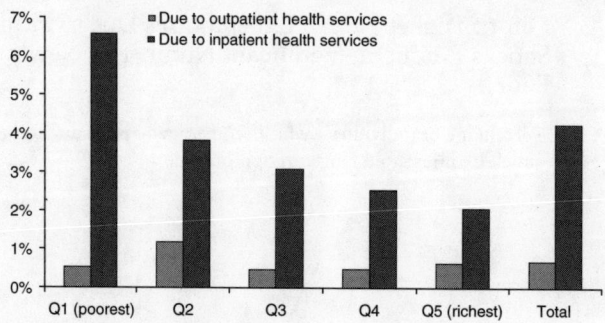

*Sources:* Knaul 2004, Bitran et al. 2004.

Ecuador 1998: Percentage of individuals who become newly poor due to a health shock by household consumption quintile

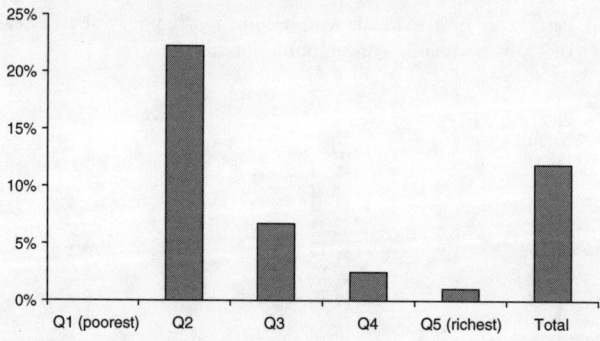

*Source:* Montenegro 2004.

*Figure 2.6* Average Previsional Household Monthly per Capita Income Pre- and Post-Out-of-Pocket Health Spending, Honduras 1998-99

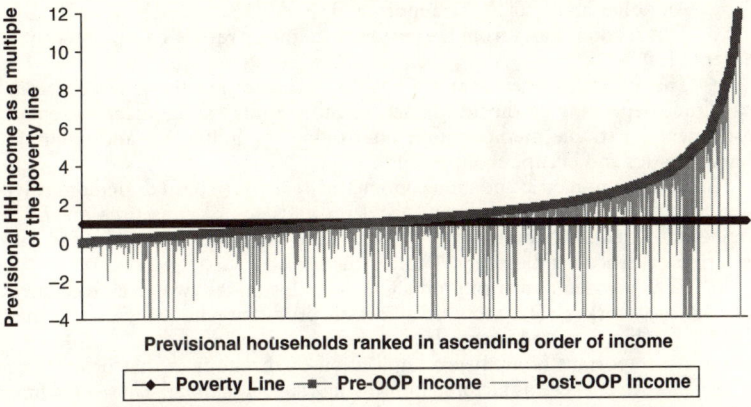

OOP=Out-of-pocket.

*Note*: This figure shows the impact of out-of-pocket expenditures every household included in LSMS data in Honduras. Note that health expenditures in many cases bring household disposable income below the poverty line.

*Source:* Fiedler 2004.

*Figure 2.7* Poverty Line, Income, and Health Expenditure in Argentina

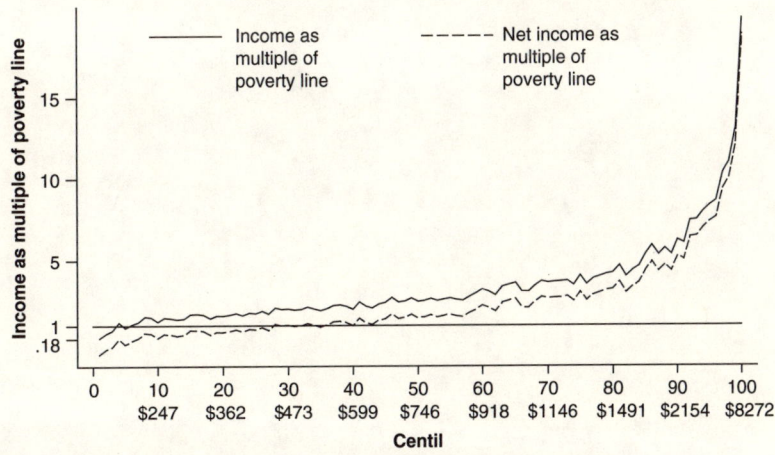

*Source:* Maceira 2004, based on ENGH97 (Argentina, National Household Expenditures Survey 1997) background paper for this publication.

# Notes

1. See, for example, Gertler and Gruber (2002) on Indonesia and other authors quoted later in this chapter.

2. All dollar amounts in this report are U.S. dollars.

3. This section draws from the extensive literature review by Montenegro and Nazerali (2004).

4. The authors suggest that although the effect of health on wages varies in magnitude depending on the health measure, the results are significant when using instrumental variable methods after controlling for individual and community characteristics and occupational profiles.

5. Both econometric and noneconometric issues have been difficult to solve—such as how to tackle endogeneity problems and lack of consensus on the best combination of anthropometric indicators. These issues must be resolved to gather empirical evidence for these labor market theories.

6. The average number of productive hours lost in the two-week recall period was 4.6 per worker. The reported losses of productive hours were not due to absenteeism but occurred in the place of work.

7. An important econometric implication of the study is that health cannot be treated as an exogenous factor in influencing wages and that the measured impact of health on wages increases tremendously when proper corrections are introduced.

8. Converting the days lost over the study period into wage-days lost per year yields a total of 16.42 wage-days lost per year, equivalent to 656.8 rupees annually.

9. PRIESO surveys were conducted in Santiago (Chile) in 2000 and Lima (Peru) in 2002. For details on Chile see Packard (2005).

# 3

# Public Policy's Role in Household Perception, Preparation, and Protection against Health Shocks

Today, after nearly two decades of sometimes bold structural reform in the health sector, the importance and financial impact of health shocks on household welfare in Latin America and the Caribbean (LAC) are clear from the empirical evidence considered in the previous chapter. Despite the diverse health finance policies and institutions in our six case study countries, three common, dramatic patterns materialize:

- Poorer households pay for a higher share of their health expenses out of pocket than the better-off, even after taking into account the expected higher demand for and consumption of health care among the well-to-do.
- Lower-income but not-yet-poor households stand the greatest likelihood of falling into poverty from out-of-pocket health expenditures, and deeper poverty is the likely impact for already poor households.
- Poor households are disproportionately represented among those whose health care depends on sometimes minimal health protection provided directly by government health ministries.

The performance of different health finance policies and institutions in providing households with financial protection will be discussed and assessed in later chapters. Here, we present a simple conceptual framework for analyzing household choices when the cost of treating illness and accidents threatens their well-being. We show how policy-relevant insights can be drawn from a conceptual look at household risk-management behavior and their implications for policy makers who want the best possible financial protection from health shocks for their people.

# Household Strategies for Managing and Coping with Shocks

Health shocks to households can undermine the health status of any household member and prevent the accumulation of human capital for many years.[1] As shown in the previous chapter, the cost of treating adverse health events can have serious repercussions on consumption and welfare, even resulting in abject poverty. Thus, as when considering other shocks to income, the classical microeconomic insurance model is helpful when examining individual and household options, incentives, and likely choices to mitigate the financial impact of adverse health events. The conceptual framework presented here is based on the classical model and drawn from the seminal paper by Ehrlich and Becker (1972). The framework has been applied to social protection policy questions related to household losses from unemployment (Gill and Ilahi 2000) and old age (Gill, Packard, and Yermo 2004).

Application of the framework begins by taking on the perspective of an individual (or household) faced with the likelihood of financial loss from an adverse event or shock. Individuals can either insure against such a loss or take steps to lower the likelihood the loss will occur. The comprehensive insurance problem of the individual (and by extension, the household) is to determine the optimal expenditure on alternative instruments—market insurance, self-insurance, and self-protection—to mitigate the loss.

Both market insurance and self-insurance transfer income from "good" to "bad" states. Where available, market insurance can be purchased at a price—the *premium,* based in classical insurance on the size and the probability of a prospective loss.[2] For self-insurance, unlike market insurance, there is no market and therefore no explicit price. However, a shadow price can be imputed from the costs an individual incurs by self-insuring. The critical difference between the two insurance instruments is that market insurance functions by pooling risk across individuals; self-insurance—essentially individual saving—does not. Individuals who—by choice or by necessity (because either or both instruments are unavailable)—neither insure through a market nor self-insure are forced to cope with losses from any bad states that occur. The third mitigation instrument, self-protection or prevention, reduces the occurrence probability of the bad state but, because it does not transfer income from good to bad states, does not affect the size of the loss if the bad state occurs.[3]

For simplicity (and to reflect the growing sophistication of the lexicon), we have replaced the terms originally used by Ehrlich and Becker. We refer to market insurance as risk pooling,[4] to self-insurance as saving, and self-protection as prevention. Thus, risk pooling (discussed in chapter 4) redistributes consumption opportunities toward the bad states at a price paid by households either directly through premiums or indirectly through general taxation. Saving redistributes income similarly—cash balances reduce fluctuations in consumption—but does not pool risks. Prevention lowers the occurrence probability of the bad state.

According to the framework, individuals or households smooth consumption over good and bad states. Where risk pooling is missing, the individual is forced to smooth consumption using only saving and prevention. In a world that offers the options of both risk pooling and saving, the individual sees these as substitutes. Risk pooling—available at or near actuarially fair prices—reduces saving. However, greater coverage of risk pooling does not inevitably result in individuals' spending less on prevention.[5] If prevention lowers the likelihood that the bad state will occur, and if this is rewarded by the market in the form of lower premiums, risk pooling and prevention can become complements, individuals can be encouraged to take up more prevention in return for cheaper risk-pooling instruments.

Figure 3.1 illustrates (though imperfectly) the prescriptions of the comprehensive insurance framework that can be drawn from our discussion thus far on just two axes, each representing different dimensions of prospective losses: size (amount of the loss) and loss frequency (occurrence probability).

From a financial protection perspective, it is more efficient for individuals to cope than try to insure against small, rarely occurring losses (figure 3.1, bottom, left corner). However, as prospective losses grow and become more frequent, it is more efficient to engage in prevention and saving to mitigate the loss (that is, to lower the probability and cover the cost). As a prospective loss becomes less frequent but increases in size, risk pooling is more efficient. For many large, rare losses, households will have incentives to engage in prevention to further lower the occurrence probability. However, for frequently occurring and catastrophic losses (figure 3.1, top, right corner), individuals, households, or markets can do little on their own.

Sickness strikes in a wide variety of conditions. Most frequent illnesses are not serious nor do they imply huge costs and financial losses. In fact, for 80–90 percent of health events that households will experience in their lifetimes, people rarely go to the doctor. Most symptoms—headaches, the common cold, adult diarrhea, and even minor fever—last for fewer than three or four days and can be easily treated with rest and nonprescription pharmaceuticals. To mitigate the financial losses from these relatively small, frequent symptoms, most households are better off with prevention (nutrition, good hygiene, preventive and primary medicine, exercise) and saving (individually assuming the cost of treatment and medication).

*Figure 3.1* Mitigation Instruments according to Size and
          Frequency of Potential Losses

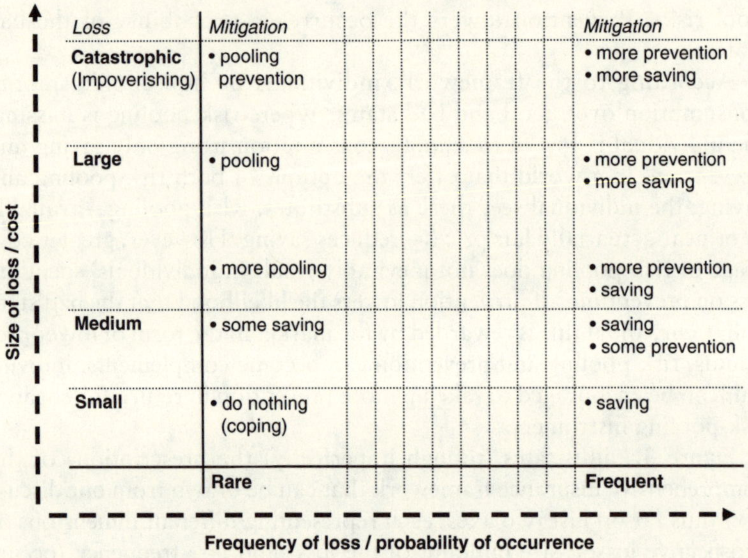

| Loss | Mitigation | | | | | | | | | | | Mitigation |
|------|-----------|--|--|--|--|--|--|--|--|--|--|-----------|
| **Catastrophic** (Impoverishing) | • pooling prevention | | | | | | | | | | | • more prevention<br>• more saving |
| **Large** | • pooling | | | | | | | | | | | • more prevention<br>• more saving |
| | • more pooling | | | | | | | | | | | • more prevention<br>• saving |
| **Medium** | • some saving | | | | | | | | | | | • saving<br>• some prevention |
| **Small** | • do nothing (coping) | | | | | | | | | | | • saving |
| | **Rare** | | | | | | | | | | | **Frequent** |

Size of loss / cost (vertical axis)

Frequency of loss / probability of occurrence (horizontal axis)

*Source:* Authors, based on Gill and Ilahi 2000.

However, for treatment of less frequently occurring, more serious
illnesses, costs can quickly mount. Indeed, for conditions such as com-
plicated flu, pneumonia, bacterial bronchitis, or urinary infections, the
cost of diagnosis, treatment, and resolution can be substantial. Medical
consultation becomes critical to identify more serious conditions. To
cover the potential financial consequences of less frequent sicknesses
that are costly to treat, households are better off increasing their participation in risk-pooling arrangements.

As potential losses from the cost of treating health events grow—
because they tend to impoverish—the need for instruments to
pool risks rapidly becomes apparent. For uncertain conditions diag-
nosed as requiring inpatient care (hospitalization)—such as serious
injury from accidents, heart attack, stroke, and renal failure—the
costs of treatment and resolution can escalate dramatically and are
difficult for most households to cover on their own. A mechanism to

pool risks for these losses becomes critical for effective financial protection.

## The Importance of Information on Household Choices to Cover Health Shocks

The prescriptions of the classical insurance model on which this framework is based are dependant on certain critical assumptions and thus somewhat vulnerable to the market failures discussed in the economics literature, where these assumptions fail to hold.[6] However, of particular concern in a discussion of risk pooling—specifically, contributory insurance arrangements—are the problems posed by imperfect information. These merit mention before we go further in applying the framework to health shocks.

For many of the classical model assumptions to hold, consumers and suppliers have to have information about the quality of available services, their price, and the likely demand for services in the future. Although households are well informed about many of the goods and services they consume (such as food and clothing), they may be less well informed about the quality of certain sophisticated goods and services. Health care is a prime example. Even where markets respond by providing information (directly to consumers or through third-party specialists for hire), the information may be too complex for consumers to grasp to make the right choices. Even with information about quality, and with new technology (mass advertising and the Internet)[7] that allows customers to be better informed, they may still not know whether they are getting the best price. Further, knowledge about future needs will always be less than complete—an information problem that in many ways motivates the market for risk-pooling instruments in the first place, but which, nonetheless, often frustrates the functioning of this market as well.

Barr (2001) points out how the information problems that confound the simple predictions of the classical insurance model and market provision of risk pooling are particularly treacherous when considering health risks and household demand for medical care. The information consumers have about their medical needs (whether they even have a health problem, what treatment they need, and how much treatment) and the quality of medical services offered is particularly poor. Knowledge is highly technical, individually specific, and therefore costly to acquire. The cost of choosing the wrong treatment or purchasing poor-quality treatment is frequently high. And uncertainty about future needs for health care is great.

## Information Problems that Plague Provision
## of Insurance Instruments

This last point shifts our discussion slightly from information problems that hinder consumer choice to those that hinder market provision of saving and risk-pooling instruments in particular. An uneven or *asymmetrical* distribution of information between consumers and providers leads to two problems that consistently plague private markets for this form of mitigation: *adverse selection* and *moral hazard*.

Adverse selection—the "hidden knowledge problem"—occurs because the consumers most eager to obtain risk-pooling services are frequently the ones likely to need them most. Individuals often know their own and their family's health needs better than do the risk-pooling providers. In a market that prices loss probability (risk-rated contributory insurance), individuals expecting losses will demand risk-pooling instruments but have a strong incentive to hide this knowledge about themselves from providers. The entry of "risky" consumers lowers the risk-pool quality, eventually forcing the insurer to raise prices. The higher price of risk pooling can put off low-risk individuals, further threatening the quality and financial viability of the risk-pooling instrument. Too many bad risks will squeeze out "winners" to finance the payout from the risk pool to the "losers" who suffer losses. This cycle poses a special challenge to social insurance–type risk-pooling arrangements and to the extension of contributory risk pooling to the informal and unsalaried population (see chapter 5).

Moral hazard—the "hidden action problem"—occurs when providers of risk-pooling instruments cannot observe consumer activities that can raise or lower the occurrence likelihood of the bad state. Risk-pooling coverage can actually give incentives for individuals and households to act—or more often fail to act—in ways that allow or force them to consume more benefits from the risk pool. If the potential payouts are great or easy to get and the insurer cannot observe the insured's behavior, these individuals will have strong incentives to provoke the payout, particularly if the (physical and psychological) costs to the individual of increasing the probability of the bad state are relatively low.[8] Paradoxically, health insurance actively increases moral hazard by design as it seeks to reduce the revealed price of health services to consumers at the point of contact.

Asymmetrical information problems are notorious for causing the contributory risk-pooling market to fail and could even prevent these markets from forming in the first place. Both adverse selection and moral hazard are frequently observed in the provision of risk-pooling mechanisms for mitigating health shocks, particularly in the provision of nonrisk-related contributory insurance.

As suggested earlier and illustrated in figure 3.1, risk-pooling mechanisms cope badly with losses that occur frequently, that is, events whose likelihood approaches certainty or events that have already occurred. The problem becomes pernicious when considering financial protection from adverse health events, many of which can become chronic conditions requiring sustained—and costly—medical attention. Because the onset of a chronic condition may be difficult to predict, it is readily insurable with risk-pooling arrangements. Once the condition strikes, it becomes preexisting and is usually excluded from risk-pooling arrangements, depending on time frames for enrollment and contributions to the risk-pooling arrangement. For example, advances in genetics put information on the probability of chronic conditions within the reach of insurers. This can increase market efficiency for private risk pooling, but it can also increase the difficulty of finding adequate financial protection for households.

Similarly, risk pooling fares poorly when the probability that one member of the risk pool will suffer losses in the bad state causes (or increases the probability of) another member to suffer the loss (that is, when the probabilities of suffering the loss are not independent). In such cases, the risk of loss is said to be "systemic" and can result in reliance by too many unlucky pool members (who suffer the bad state) on the premium of too few lucky members (who stay healthy). Certain health events—even those that are costly to treat—can occur frequently. Further, the threats to good health, and thus the probability of health shocks, are often difficult to isolate and contain. A notable example is malaria, an endemic condition in many parts of the world.

But what about the other protective instrument households have—self-insurance or individual saving? The discussion so far has been contained to information problems for risk-pooling instruments. Risk pooling and saving are substitutes. Relatively predictable or certain events (with which risk pooling copes badly) are best mitigated through individual saving. However, many of these same problems—as well as additional factors particular to health shocks and the medical market—complicate the prescription of saving instruments to cover relatively predictable financial losses from health events.

Even if adverse health events are relatively predictable and losses are relatively small, a lack of information can still lead consumers to make poor, costly, and even irrevocable choices. Moreover, as the losses implied by predictable events grow, the stress, anxiety, and urgency that accompany adverse health events can dramatically limit the amount of shopping individuals can do, further hindering consumer choice.

Finally, even modest charges for treatment of predictable health problems have been shown to lower consumption of critically important care, particularly among lower-income groups (Gertler and Van der Gaag 1988; Bitran and McInnes 1993). Failure to purchase treatment for relatively predictable, minor events can cause what would have been small losses to grow rapidly.

The information problems discussed here are serious caveats to prescriptions for a comprehensive insurance framework to mitigate losses from health events, particularly in the availability of risk-pooling instruments. These problems and wider market failures lead to inefficiencies that can raise the price of mitigation mechanisms out of the reach of lower-income groups and above what is economically viable, thus conspiring to create gaps in financial protection. Often these gaps are among population groups who most need protection, such as the elderly, expectant mothers and children, and the chronically ill.

In light of this discussion, how then do households manage health shocks? Do their preferences, choices, and actions follow the predictions of the comprehensive insurance model presented earlier? Do the information problems—and other market failures discussed—explain household choices that seemingly depart from what the framework would predict? Unfortunately, few data are available in LAC countries that would allow analysis that provides even preliminary answers to these questions. Figure 3.2 shows how households in Chile reported dealing with health shocks that forced them to lose income, incur substantial costs, or both, because they either did not participate in any risk-pooling mechanisms or the mechanism was insufficient to protect them from excess expenditures.

We have presented a conceptual framework based on the classical economic insurance model and explained how the framework can be used to prescribe the optimal combination of risk-mitigating strategies and instruments to minimize prospective losses from unexpected adverse events. We have also reviewed well-known limitations of the classical model on which the conceptual framework is based and shown how insidious they are, especially when considering losses from health shocks. In light of these shortcomings, can the framework be at all useful as a guide for formulating policy?

The limitations that confound the classical insurance model on which our framework is based usually mean that one or more of the mitigation instruments—risk pooling, individual saving, or prevention—is unavailable to households or that households are forced to choose a less-than-optimal instrument. Indeed, the role of the policy maker and of government is to augment household options where any of the mitigation instruments are unavailable or out of reach.

*Figure 3.2* Sources of Household Savings to Manage Income
Shocks from Adverse Health Events and the Cost
of Care When Risk Pooling Fails, Chile

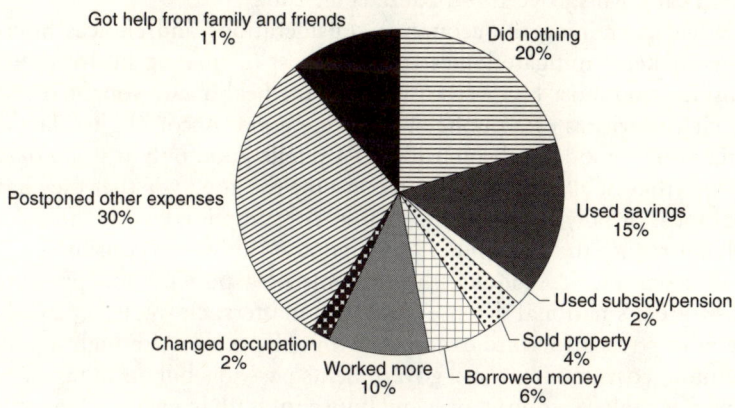

*Note:* Responses to the question, "How did you manage losses from the
[health] shock?"
*Source:* Bitran, Giedion, and Muñoz 2004 with data from PRIESO, Chile
2000.

The acknowledged lack of efficient instruments for financial protection in most LAC countries is sufficient evidence of a need for policy
intervention. Many of the problems observed in LAC today that limit
effective financial protection, however, are symptoms of policies formu-
lated without the insurance framework in mind. The existence of market
failures and information gaps indicates *whether* governments should be
involved in helping to augment household options to manage the risks of
financial losses from costly health shocks. The comprehensive insurance
framework indicates *how* government should get involved. This involve-
ment can be through direct public provision, the regulation of private
provision, and subsidies. Disregard of the framework, and the tested
principles on which it is based, by policy makers when crafting policies
can lead to further distortions and do more damage than good.

## The Role of Public Policy in Protecting Households
from the Impoverishing Effects of Health Shocks

Now we will extend our conceptual framework to further accommodate
the particular and demanding aspects of health shocks and use it to tease

out what the essential role of public policy is in augmenting households' instruments for managing these shocks. But first we should capture a market peculiarity that is relevant to any discussion of the risk of adverse health: the public good and externality dimensions of good health and health care (Musgrove 1996; Baeza et al. 2002).

When examining the economic considerations and choices households make to mitigate losses from the cost of treating health events, consideration must be given to whether the health care sought reflects the characteristics of a public or a private good. According to classical definition, a good can be considered a public good only if it is *nonexclusive* (that is, all individuals can consume the good whether they have paid for it or not) and *nonrival* (that is, consumption by one individual will not reduce the availability of the good for others to consume).

In economics textbooks, the example of a public good presented most often is national defense. In health matters, clean air is probably the most straightforward example of a public good. Although fighting pollution costs money—and governments pass this bill on to taxpayers —policy makers cannot prevent households that evade taxes from breathing clean air, nor does the clean air consumed by a particular household make less air available for others. In contrast, health interventions that are private goods in the economic sense are available only to individuals who pay for them and their consumption implies a reduction of the number available to others, such as cosmetic surgery. For example, restricting consumption of nose surgery for cosmetic reasons to individuals who pay for it would be easy, and a household's consumption of this treatment makes less of the surgeon's time available for others.

However, the medical market abounds in examples of goods (treatments and interventions) that bear all the characteristics of private goods (they are excludable and their consumption is rival) but clearly affect the welfare of other individuals than the person treated. When left to pure market forces, economic theory predicts that from society's perspective, private goods that have these positive external effects (*externalities*) will always be underconsumed (similarly, private goods with negative externalities will always be overconsumed). In other words, consumption of these goods will not be optimal from society's perspective, and underconsumption could jeopardize the greater good.

Immunization is a particularly good example of a health intervention with private good characteristics at low coverage, but unambiguous and powerful social benefits at high coverage (*herd immunity*). When immunization coverage is high enough (usually more than 80 percent of the susceptible population), no epidemic of the disease is likely to occur (for example, measles). So the benefits of vaccinated children will extend to the unvaccinated. But this example comes with a word of caution: below a sufficient coverage level (for example, leaving 30 percent of the population at risk), vaccines are pure private goods, because only the vaccinated child is likely to be protected from the disease or an epidemic. Thus, the societal importance of reaching vaccination threshold coverage is enormous. The use of condoms is another good example of private goods with substantial societal benefits, because they protect not only the person using them but also his sexual partner, thus lowering the spread of sexually transmitted diseases.

Thus, a third dimension (figure 3.3) is added to considerations of the nature of prospective losses—size of loss and cost (figure 3.1) and frequency and probability of occurrence. This is the degree of externality or extent of social benefit conferred or loss imposed on others by many health treatments and interventions of a public-good nature, even some that are clearly private goods. In other words, the degree of externality arising from intervening (or failing to intervene) in the loss presents an additional and powerful justification for public policy or state intervention.

Figure 3.3 illustrates these three dimensions of our adapted conceptual framework and also includes households' and policy makers' options for covering financial losses from health shocks. The admittedly simplistic, yet powerful, policy prescriptions discussed above become dramatically clear. The size and frequency of the prospective loss determines whether these are best mitigated by risk pooling, individual saving, prevention, or all three (and the relative weight assigned each instrument). Regardless of the instrument, however, moving along the third dimension away from the origin, the externality posed by the prospective loss grows, and the justification increases for government intervention to ensure the appropriate action. For ease of interpretation, we have illustrated these three dimensions using a cube.

There is a fourth dimension to the discussion of household management of health shocks, health, and health care: the cost-effectiveness of treatment. Risk pooling, saving, and prevention could all be available, and households are likely to make sensible decisions about which instruments to employ to cover the prospective costs of a given health event. However, one or all of these instruments could finance health interventions that are ineffective, or if effective, so expensive as to outweigh the treatment benefits. A household may decide to spend so much on an ineffective intervention that it ends up consuming a large part of household income and increasing the risk of household poverty.

The history of medical practice is replete with these kinds of examples. Instead of subsidizing a household for an ineffective or impoverishing intervention, government needs to educate providers and

*Figure 3.3* Capturing the Public Goods Dimension:
Characteristics of Health Shocks and Policy
Implications in the Comprehensive Insurance
Framework

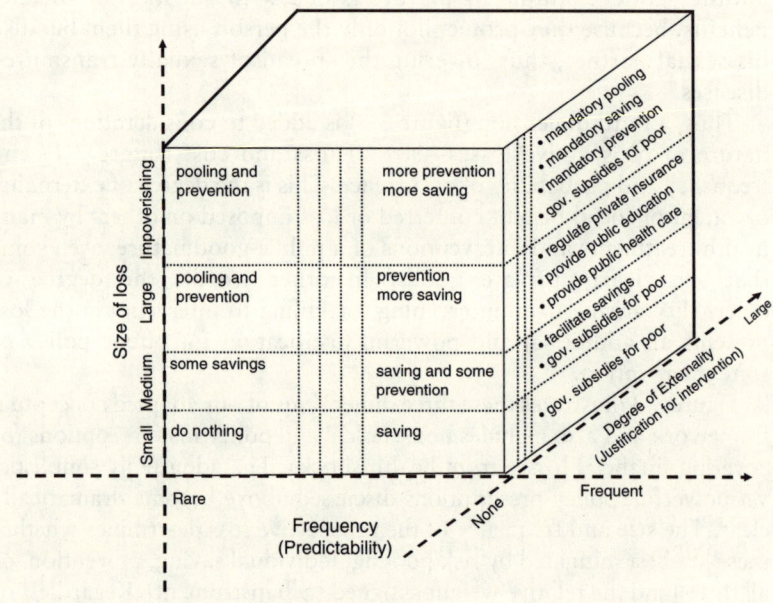

*Sources:* Authors based on Gill and Ilahi 2000 and Baeza et al. 2002.

households on the ineffectiveness of these practices and ensure
that medical care meets standards of proven (evidence-based)
effectiveness.

Therefore, to focus this discussion specifically on health finance concerns, public financing is advisable both for cost-effective measures and
treatments that have characteristics of public goods and for cost-effective
services that have characteristics of private goods and important externalities. Due to the characteristics of public goods and externalities, public
financing is important to avoid the risks to a population's health that in-
appropriate consumption might cause—with reference to the framework,
this is an example of society-level prevention. The cost of publicly financing such services is offset by the benefit of avoiding these risks. Indeed, to
the extent that investment in prevention can lower the incidence of more
serious health events, these measures can lower future expenditure from
the risk pool.

## The Government's Role in Augmenting Household Risk Management, Financial Protection, and Health Outcomes

The negative impact of health shocks on both health status and nonmedical consumption can have a detrimental long-term impact on human capital and can perpetuate poverty. Thus, public policy in health should be directed toward maintaining and improving health status through cost-effective public health interventions and widespread use of medical services. But policy makers also have the more difficult task of achieving this goal while ensuring financial protection for households. Table 3.1, derived from figure 3.3, summarizes some of the main strategies government has used to achieve this goal.

An excessive household health expenditure can result from the cost of treating acute or chronic health conditions, but can also result from the financial burden of contributing to a risk-pooling scheme. In this regard, we should be concerned not just about excess out-of-pocket expenditures and their negative consequences on use of services, disposable income, and human capital creation (chapter 2). We should also consider the overall financial burden on individuals and households that may include payments to a risk-pooling scheme. Those, too, can be financially catastrophic over the short or long haul.

In most arenas, households are "context takers," while policy makers are "context setters." In few arenas is this more apparent than in health care and in household considerations of how to finance the care they need. Unlike other prospective losses to income that threaten household welfare (for example, unemployment and old age), losses from health events often demand immediate attention from policy makers due to the prevalence of market failures and information gaps in the medical market and to the many public-good features and externalities of good health and health care. Just because the need for policy intervention is more immediate, however, does not mean that policy makers can forget sound economic principles for best managing risks and covering prospective losses.

Governments in LAC do not lack enthusiasm about intervening in areas where private agents fear to tread. LAC experience with public interventions in health has been long and rich, particularly with public and quasi-public risk-pooling mechanisms based on Bismarckian principles of labor regulation and taxation. In many ways, governments in LAC countries took steps ahead of the United States and other Organisation for Economic Co-operation and Development (OECD) member countries. The LAC region also has extensive experience with Beveridge-type arrangements. Sometimes, however, eagerness to intervene has overridden careful consideration of how best to intervene.

*Table 3.1* Government's Risk-Mitigation Instruments for Helping Households Manage Financial Losses from Adverse Health Events

| Type of Household Loss | Household Strategy | Government Strategy |
|---|---|---|
| Rare, impoverishing | Pooling<br>Prevention | Mandate pooling<br>Implement prevention interventions<br>Provide public subsidies |
| Rare, large | Pooling<br>Some saving | Promote and regulate mandatory and voluntary insurance |
| Rare, medium | Some saving | Facilitate saving (develop financial markets) |
| Rare, small | Do nothing | Do nothing |
| Frequent, impoverishing | Saving<br>Prevention | Mandate saving<br>Prevention<br>Direct subsidies |
| Frequent, large | Saving<br>Prevention | Facilitate and regulate saving (financial markets) |
| Frequent, medium | Saving<br>Prevention | Facilitate saving |
| Frequent, medium and small | Some saving | Facilitate saving |
| Public goods and private goods with externalities, or both | n.a. | Provide full public financing of interventions |
| Ineffective health interventions | n.a. | Educate providers and households |

n.a.=Not applicable.
*Source:* Derived from figure 3.3.

72

A core problem of policy intervention in health finance—especially in public or publicly mandated risk-pooling mechanisms—is misalignment of instruments (risk pooling, saving, and prevention) with respect to the likelihood and cost of successfully treating most adverse health events. This misalignment is manifest in at least five features of health finance systems in the LAC region:

- High household out-of-pocket expenditures in relation to total health expenditures in most countries, but particularly the poorest ones
- Frequent inclusion of nonimpoverishing private goods in publicly subsidized care
- Inclusion of public goods in mandated risk-pooling mechanisms (such as social insurance [SI] or mandatory private insurance)[9]
- Failure to include what are clearly insurable interventions (low-probability, high-cost interventions) in mandatory social or private risk pooling
- Inclusion of uninsurables (certain high-probability, high-cost interventions) in risk-pooling packages.

Concrete country examples of each of these misalignments and the distortions they cause are readily available. In Argentina, the quasi-public *Obras Sociales* has long been mandated to include vaccination—an obvious public-prevention measure with large positive externalities—in its package of care, but there has been too little take up. In 1997, Obras Sociales showed significantly lower vaccination coverage than the Ministry of Health. The mandatory private risk-pooling providers in Chile (Instituciones de Salud Previsional did not effectively cover catastrophic events (for example, chronic renal failure and transplant, and some cancer treatments) until recently (2000). Lack of coverage for these low-probability events that are costly to treat forces thousands of households to rely on the public national health fund, Fondo Nacional de Salud for coverage or on their own out-of-pocket payment. Finally, almost every country in the world mandates contributory risk-pooling plans (for example, SI and private providers of mandatory health insurance) to cover normal delivery (childbirth). A normal delivery may be an admittedly costly but wholly predictable health event that is often initiated knowingly and willingly by fertile couples. Therefore, it would be more effectively covered through savings—or through direct public subsidies in the likely case it is a potentially impoverishing event for lower-income households.

This last example will surprise many readers in light of the justified policy preoccupation with safe childbirth in almost every country. Considering the social importance of safe childbirth, how can the inclusion of normal child delivery possibly be considered a misalignment? Normal childbirth is almost a certainty among young couples and women of many socioeconomic backgrounds. Less predictable are the *complications* of pregnancy. The first event—pregnancy and childbirth—is highly predictable and thus, according to the framework presented in this chapter, is best covered by individual savings. The second event—*complications* in pregnancy and childbirth—is unpredictable and therefore perfectly insurable. The misalignment arises from the failure to distinguish between the two prospective financial losses by public regulators as well as by public and quasi-public risk-pooling mechanisms.

We do not necessarily suggest that policy makers should drop normal delivery coverage from insurance packages. There may be noneconomic reasons for including this care in insurance plans. However, policy makers need to be aware of the efficiency and equity consequences of the perverse incentives created by this misalignment for both providers and consumers of insurance.

Each example of misalignment discussed above is partially a symptom of a sectorwide aversion among health specialists to view individual saving as a legitimate and effective part of the array of instruments that households can use to manage losses from health shocks. With the exception of deductibles and copayment arrangements within risk-pooling systems—intended largely as a means of controlling overconsumption of health care spurred by moral hazard—health specialists frequently reject individual saving outright as a legitimate financing instrument. This aversion stems from legitimate concerns that households should not have to pay for care out-of-pocket at the moment they need care, when they have little time to "shop," and the psychological costs (desperation) make acquiring care paramount, particularly among the poor.

However, upon closer examination of the antisavings arguments in health policy circles, what is really at issue among health specialists is not the individualization of financing for predictable events (even costly predictable events). The issue lies in protecting households from having to pay the cost of care at the very moment they need medical attention. In short, the issue is one of timing. Policy makers in health circles are not prejudiced against saving per se, but want to ensure an adequate degree of prepayment. Transferring resources from good times to bad times is the essence of saving and, with the right macroeconomic policies and regulations, the financial sector can meet this need by providing access to credit and other savings instruments. This insight points to a need for a wider and increasingly sophisticated array of contractual savings and other financial instruments and forges a critical link between the policy agendas in health social protection and financial sector development.

But why should households be forced to navigate the complex territory of sophisticated financial instruments, when the state can include anything and everything in the risk pool, and thereby guarantee the maximum possible prepayment? In risk-pooling systems that cover everybody, this is admittedly less problematic, although the distortions in the wider economy from the high taxes needed to finance a health insurance system that covers uninsurable events cannot be dismissed. However, in Latin America's fragmented risk-pooling systems, where different households are covered by different arrangements, financing the cost of treating uninsurable (largely predictable) events out of the risk-pooling system can often imply that limited resources are consumed too quickly by too few, leaving too many—often the poorest—to face the cost of truly insurable events out-of-pocket. As seen in chapter 2, this outcome can lead to impoverishment or deepen the poverty of the already poor.

We will return to the discussion of how best to structure risk-pooling plans and just what these plans—as instruments in the broader health-finance architecture—need to cover. Chapter 2 presented evidence of household impoverishment by health shocks—particularly households in the lower-income distribution quintiles. But why should households suffer health shock impoverishment when they are, at least in theory, covered by health care and health finance arrangements? Households in every country examined can—at the very least—rely on national health care delivered directly by ministries of health.

Now we have begun to venture a controversial hypothesis in response to this question: namely, that more households would benefit from effective financial protection if the instruments government puts at their disposal were correctly aligned. If these instruments were better matched to the nature of the losses in question, not only would the health finance system be more effective at helping households cover the costs of care, but public resources might also be freed to finance subsidies to the poor or near-poor who cannot afford to use the instruments of contributory risk pooling, saving, or prevention.

## Household Coping Strategies

To close this section of our discussion of policy interventions to help households manage losses from the cost of care after a health shock, we turn briefly to the action households are most likely to take up for want of any other option: *coping*. As seen from the evidence presented in the previous chapter, a portion of household out-of-pocket spending on health care is entirely appropriate—to treat relatively small, frequently occurring, uninsurable health events with no clear externalities. However, a substantial share of this spending goes to finance rare, costly, insurable events that are eligible for pooling. It is this portion of out-of-pocket spending that is most likely to determine whether a household is plunged into poverty. Where insurance instruments are missing or all but inaccessible, households have little choice but to cope as best they can. Coping becomes the default, residual strategy when all other strategies—prevention, saving, and pooling—are insufficient, exhausted, or inaccessible.

Examples of "bad coping" abound. A school-age child might be pulled from her studies and be required to work to help her family pay for health care. A household may choose to forgo critical spending on food or illness prevention to make ends meet, thus increasing the likelihood of further sickness. Or a self-employed household head might have to sell an instrument or piece of machinery needed to earn a living. As stated earlier, the policy objective of financial protection is to prevent bad coping that depletes a household's reserves of human capital. Because full insurance is neither realistic nor economically efficient, even for highly risk-averse individuals, households will always engage in some coping. Just as with pooling, saving, and prevention, the role of policy makers is to ensure that a household's coping options are augmented.

Personal bankruptcy regulation, seemingly unrelated to health finance, is one important way governments can help households augment their coping options.[10] In the United States, half the people who filed for bankruptcy in 2001 did so because of health-related shocks and expenses (Himmelstein et al. 2005). This highlights the prevalence of coping in the face of health costs, even in wealthy countries. In OECD countries, a clear set of guidelines for personal bankruptcy allows households to come up with a recovery plan that is reviewed by their creditors, approved by legal authorities, and allows them to write off some of their debts and pay off others in an orderly process that improves their chances of making a fresh start. Thus, a sound personal bankruptcy regime can have profound consequences for a household's recovery from catastrophic health costs and reentering the credit market. Araujo and Funchal (2005) argue that Latin American governments still have much to do to improve their bankruptcy codes for households and firms. The authors point out that the bankruptcy process is slower and more costly in LAC than in other regions and increases the cost of credit.

## Policy Lessons from Earlier Applications of the Comprehensive Insurance Framework to Other Losses

As mentioned in the first section of this chapter, the comprehensive insurance framework has been applied on several prior occasions to examine household choices in the face of prospective losses and to form the role of public policy.

The rationale for policy intervention arises when individuals fail to attain optimal levels of risk pooling, saving, and prevention. This could be either because one or more of the instruments are not available to the individual or, if all three instruments are available, because markets are inefficient (information gaps and other market failures prevent individuals from using each instrument optimally). Gill and Ilahi (2000) draw four arguments for policy that apply irrespective of the particular prospective loss under consideration (for example, unemployment, old age, disability, or adverse health):

• *Government can provide (or help provide) instruments that the market cannot (or will not) provide.* Risk pooling to cover certain risks (for example, unemployment, poverty, disasters, and certain frequently occurring or preexisting health events with catastrophic costs) does not exist in many contexts due to information shortcomings. Government can step in to correct market failures by providing risk-pooling instruments where the private market does not.

• *Government can provide (or help provide) superior instruments where only inferior instruments are available.* For risks best covered with individual savings, private agents may turn to "bad" savings instruments (for example, using cattle, land or other illiquid assets as a medium of precautionary saving) because "good" instruments (such as diversified financial assets, safe and reliable forms of liquid savings, or credit) are not available. Furthermore, poorer households may simply not have the margin to save. Government can intervene to foster the development of more efficient instruments for saving through prudential regulation of private capital and greater access to credit markets, as well as provide direct subsidies for households too poor to hold savings or debt. This insight entails a strong link between financial sector development and social protection and health policy agendas.

• *Government can help households build and protect their human capital.* Investing in human capital—education, hygiene, and primary and preventive health care—can be an effective and powerful means of prevention. Better educated individuals are more likely to invest in preventive activities, such as exercise, as well as seek preventive health care (regular physical examinations). Healthy individuals are less likely to be unable to work, and better educated or trained workers may be less likely to suffer long-term unemployment. However, where credit is constrained, individuals may choose lower-than-optimal holdings of human capital in favor of assets with greater collateral value. To prevent individuals and households from tilting their portfolios away from human capital, government can subsidize its acquisition through public spending on education and health.

• It is usually better to help households mitigate losses than cope with them, but government can play a role in ensuring good coping. The instruments for individuals and governments to pool risks and save are not always available. The resources to take preventive measures are often scarce. Where individuals and governments are constrained, bad coping in the short run can result in longer-term detriment to household human capital. Some prevention and insurance is always desirable. Effective policy should place greater emphasis on enabling individuals to insure against losses through risk pooling and individual saving—and lower the probability of losses through prevention, rather than coping with losses after a shock. However, government can facilitate coping so that long-term detriment to human capital is minimized and households are given an adequate opportunity to recover, for example, through sound personal bankruptcy regulation.

In earlier applications of the framework, policy insights have also been gained by casting the policy maker as the risk-mitigating agent of interest. Just as individuals and households facing the prospect of a loss can pool risks, save, take preventive measures where these instruments are available, or cope with a loss should they fail to insure, governments face the same decision.

Governments can pool the risks of a limited range of possible losses through private insurance (for example, against losses from adverse climactic events, commodity crop failures, and even financial crises); save by accumulating surpluses in good times to spend on social programs during bad times (for example, through earmarking, stabilization funds, and countercyclical spending policies); and prevent poverty by practicing prudent monetary and fiscal policy, engaging in reforms that increase the efficiency and safety of factor markets, and investing in vector goods or public goods with clear, positive externalities in health.

The optimal mix of instruments governments can put in place is ultimately determined by a country's "insurance fundamentals." These are the macroeconomic, microeconomic, and sector-specific circumstances resulting from past policies, as well as factors outside policy makers' domains. A country's insurance fundamentals are: the likelihood of facing systemic crises, given its track-record of preventive adjustments, reforms, and sector policies, and its institutional and administrative capacity to identify and correct market failures and appropriately price the income risks covered by publicly provided risk-pooling mechanisms.

These assembled criteria will indicate which interventions will be most effective—augmenting private insurance options through public forms of risk pooling, augmenting individual savings through mandatory private individual accounts and improved access to credit, or a combination thereof—and the relative weight given to each. Augmenting individual and household capacity to mitigate the risk of falling into poverty in the wake of an adverse shock will increase a country's general welfare.

# Notes

1. This section draws extensively from a novel application of the classical insurance model to social protection policy questions, presented in Gill and Ilahi (2000) and extended in de Ferranti et al. (2000).

2. Conventionally, the price of market insurance $\pi$ is said to be "actuarially fair" if $\pi_i = (1 + \alpha)p_i L$, where $p_i L$ is the expected loss (that is, size of the loss $L$, weighted by probability $p$ of the loss's occurring) in the bad state, and $\alpha$ is a "loading" charged by the market-insurance provider to cover administrative costs and profit (Ehrlich and Becker 1972; Barr 2001).

3. The authors admit that, "... it is somewhat artificial to distinguish behavior that reduces the probability of the loss from behavior that reduces the size of a loss, since many actions do both" (Ehrlich and Becker 1972, 634). However, they find it helpful to separate self-protection from self-insurance because the latter clearly performs the insurance function of redistributing income from good to bad states.

4. This terminology partly reflects evolution in the literature since the Ehrlich and Becker paper. It is preferred because not all risk-pooling arrangements are market based or government provided.

5. Economists refer to this outcome as *moral hazard,* discussed later. The authors define moral hazard as an alleged deterrent effect of market insurance on self-protection that increases the probabilities of hazardous events. Much of the literature after Ehrlich and Becker (1972) has focused on adverse selection and moral hazard, for example, Marshall (1976), Hirshleifer and Riley (1979), and Coate (1995).

6. Briefly, these include imperfect competition, increasing returns to scale, credit constraints, and others discussed later at length.

7. There are studies that show that households in industrial countries increasingly consult the Internet for quality and price information for many health procedures. A report released in 2002 shows that 70 million Americans have used the Internet to acquire health information and that up to 6 million use the Internet daily for this purpose (*Economist,* July 17, 2004).

8. For example, because the physical and psychological costs of jumping into the path of a speeding car are high, the risk is low that an individual will do that to provoke a payoff from the risk pool.

9. In terms of public goods, health economics theory suggests that such interventions should be directly financed with public funds to avoid problems in the supply and demand of such services. The inclusion of such services through risk-pooling arrangements, in particular through contributory health insurance financed via payroll taxes or premiums, may have negative consequences on the efficiency of demand for and delivery of such services.

10. We are grateful to Indermit Gill for pointing out this important example of household coping after costly health shocks.

# 4

# The Role of Alternative
# Risk-Pooling Arrangements

RISK POOLING IS AN ESSENTIAL TOOL for helping households and policy makers mitigate the financial effects of health shocks, thus lowering the risk of poverty.

Societies have different ways of organizing risk-pooling systems, as discussed in chapter 1. In this chapter, we argue that the internal functional characteristics of risk pooling, more than the specific arrangements for pooling, determine its effectiveness as a risk-protection tool. Among these characteristics are a well-defined benefits package (BP) a sufficiently large pool to spread risk, the use of strategic purchasing, and the availability and portability of equity subsidies. The preliminary evidence that exists of the likely determinants of performance emerges from considerable experience with administering and reforming risk-pooling structures in Latin America and the Caribbean (LAC).

## Society's Need for Financial Protection

Households and policy makers have alternative options for protection against the risk of a health shock and the actual shock. They can reduce the probability that the shock will come about (prevention), self-insure to smooth the consumption impacts of the shock (saving), or participate in risk-pooling mechanisms. These options have been discussed in earlier chapters.

Here we consider the role of health system financing, particularly risk pooling, in ensuring financial protection, its importance in combating poverty, and some key determinants of effective performance. We focus especially on risk pooling for three main reasons. First, although alternatives exist and indeed are desirable, risk pooling is the largest and main public policy intervention to help households protect themselves against health care costs. Second, uncertain insurable health care costs, due to their size and unexpected nature, are the most likely to throw households into poverty (and the poor or near-poor into abject poverty), although uninsurable events can also do so. Because these events are best mitigated through risk pooling, a discussion of how risk-pooling functions in a country is a clear link between the health and poverty-prevention policy agendas. Third, LAC structural reforms in the health sector in the last 20 years have been focused almost exclusively on improving the functioning of risk-pooling instruments (discussed in chapter 6).

To provide effective options for protecting households against the consequences of health shocks, policy makers must make two key decisions about the source and volume of financing and about the organizational arrangements. How the system is financed largely determines the system's capacity to improve people's health and protect them financially. Effective arrangements ensure funding for health interventions and medical services and also create the right incentive framework for both consumers and providers of those services. These arrangements contribute to financial protection by promoting the use of the right financing strategy, particularly pooling financial contributions for uncertain and large financial losses (insurable events, as discussed in chapter 3) so that all members of the pool, not each contributor individually, bear the financial risk.

Ensuring financial protection means that no household should fall into poverty or be further impoverished from its health care contributions and expenditures. As discussed in chapter 2, empirical evidence shows that high contributions (taxes, premiums) as well as out-of-pocket health expenditures can drive disposable income below the poverty line, forcing households to cut back on food and other goods and services vital to their well-being.

In addition to providing enough funding to run the health care system, ensuring that a health system provides financial protection requires:

• Achieving the highest degree possible of contribution for insurable health events before services are needed (prepayment). This should help decrease out-of-pocket payments (the contribution at the moment services are needed), even with the use of copayments when evidence of overuse may exist.
• Achieving the largest possible risk pool within a population, or at least ensuring sufficiently large risk pools to be financially viable. This should allow transfer of subsidies from lower-risk to higher-risk individuals (risk subsidy).
• Achieving adequate equity to ensure a reasonable flow of subsidies between higher-income groups to lower-income groups (equity subsidization).

• Developing purchasing capacity and a provider-payment system that creates incentives for providers to deliver quality health services in a timely manner while keeping costs down (strategic purchasing).

Achieving these objectives depends on how well health systems arrange the three main health financing functions discussed in chapter 1 (WHO 2000): revenue collection, risk pooling, and purchasing. Although each of these functions plays an important role in ensuring financial protection for households, risk pooling, and correctly structuring the pool's risk subsidy, plays a central role.

## The Importance of a Mandatory Benefits Package

For sound public policy in health, establishing a mandatory BP is essential, no matter what type of risk-pooling arrangements are put in place. The BP defines the interventions covered and the financial and quality conditions of coverage. To provide effective financial protection, the package has to be concentrated around impoverishing events.

Public subsidies are justified to forestall health event–generated poverty. Should society therefore subsidize any intervention a household demands in response to a health shock that may throw them into poverty? Fiscal constraints limit government's capacity to subsidize households. Even if there were no fiscal constraints, however, households might demand ineffective health interventions due to information asymmetry or incomplete knowledge.

In addition, in the absence of a BP, public subsidization of households based exclusively on households' paying for services that could plunge them into poverty can result in regressive subsidization. Rich households, demanding complex and expensive interventions (with no limit), could also argue that they are at risk of impoverishment, because most public subsidies with a significant opportunity cost for society are concentrated on subsidizing the poor for simple and often highly cost-effective interventions. Tax incentives for health insurance (frequent in the LAC region) are often put in place without any BP. This signifies that society is willing to subsidize any consumption regardless of the services demanded or the income of the household receiving the subsidy. The adequate policy response for the rich household case is to promote voluntary private health insurance.

Finally, the current mandatory contribution to social security in health (payroll tax) in the absence of a BP becomes a mandate for expenditure rather than insurance protection, with significantly perverse incentives for households and risk-pooling organizations alike. Such incentives and the difficulties of extending contributory risk pooling to workers in the informal sector are discussed in chapter 5.

## Risk Pooling in Latin America and the Caribbean

Figures 4.1 and 4.2 show the coverage of alternative risk-pooling arrangements from two different perspectives. Figure 4.1 shows how the population of each country in our case studies is distributed between the different forms of coverage. Figure 4.2 shows this distribution by household income quintile. Immediately evident is that poorer households are covered only by the national health services provided by their countries' ministries of health (MOHs) and financed from general taxation. This fact in itself need not necessarily imply coverage of lesser quality—as demonstrated by the care provided in the United Kingdom's National Health Service or the Swedish national health system, which are open to all and financed from general revenue. What matters is whether existing risk-pooling organizations are efficient in providing access to effective and needed health services and financial protection. However, in many LAC countries, the problems that compromise effectiveness and quality in public health systems in industrial countries are compounded by much smaller budgets, greater scarcity and rationing, greater lack of administrative capacity, isolation of rural populations, and corruption. Often, these problems also affect social insurance arrangements in the LAC region.

## What Arrangement Gives the Best Financial Protection?

Evidence has been scarce for comparing the performance of alternative risk-pooling arrangements by health status (or use of services) and financial protection. Evidence from our country cases suggests that there are indeed differences but that they are related more to specific internal functional characteristics within each risk-pooling arrangement than to whether it is a Bismarck- or a Beveridge-type arrangement. Evidence from Colombia and Chile presented in this section supports this point.

In 1994, Colombia introduced explicit insurance BPs: one for formal workers (Régimen Contributivo) and one for the population under the Régimen Subsidiado. There is no explicit package as yet for the population under the MOH, the *vinculados*. A transition from traditional national health services to the new Régimen Subsidiado has taken place, which in

*Figure 4.1* Coverage by Risk-Pooling Arrangement
(percentage of the population)

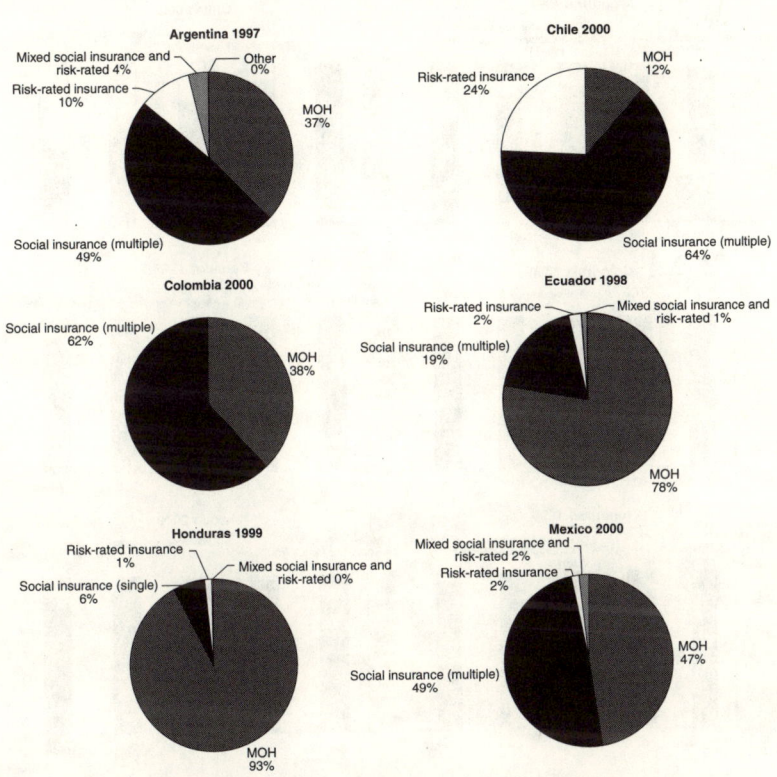

MOH=Ministry of health.

*Note:* Households in higher-income countries are covered mostly by social security or private insurance. In lower-income countries, they are covered mostly by national health services.

a. Multiple social insurance in Chile includes Fondo Nacional de Salud (FONASA) and the armed forces and police systems.

*Sources:* Background papers developed for this study, Chile and Colombia, Bitran et al. 2004; Honduras, Fiedler 2004; Mexico, Knaul et al. 2004; Argentina, Maceira 2004; and Ecuador, Montenegro 2004.

*Figure 4.2* Coverage by Risk-Pooling Mechanism,
by Household Income Quintile

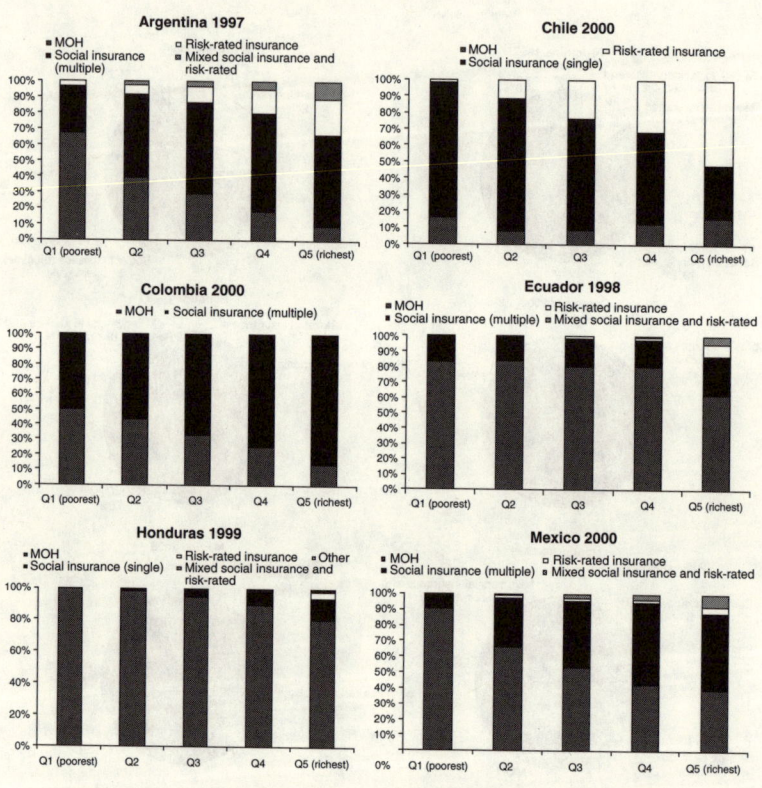

MOH=Ministry of Health.

*Note:* Lower-income groups rely more on national health provision from the ministries of health. Higher-income groups are covered by social security and private insurance.

*Source:* See figure 4.1.

practice has meant the existence of three risk-pooling arrangements. Colombia also introduced a demand-side subsidy for the Régimen Subsidiado, funded mostly, but not exclusively, from general taxation.

The Régimen Subsidiado performs better on financial protection than the traditional national health service (MOH) arrangement. Figure 4.3

*Figure 4.3* Impoverishment Incidence among Inpatients and
Outpatients, Colombia, 2003

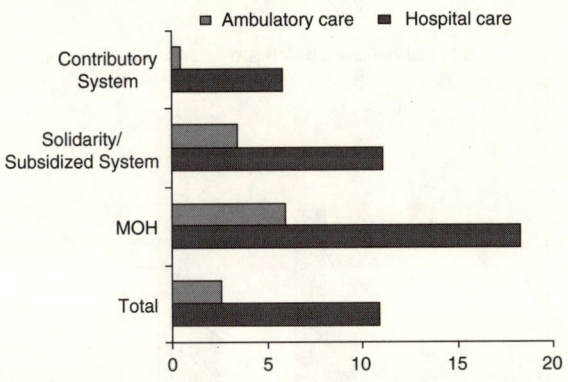

MOH=Ministry of health.
*Note:* In Colombia, the Régimen Subsidiado outperforms national health
services in financial protection.
*Source:* Bitran et al. 2004.

shows that 17 percent of households facing a health shock requiring
inhospital care covered by the national health service fell into poverty,
but this happened to only 11 percent and 6 percent of the people
covered, respectively, by the Régimen Subsidiado and the Régimen
Contributivo. A similar phenomenon occurs for health shocks requiring
ambulatory care, though of lesser magnitude due to the usually lower
cost of such care. In this case, the incidence of impoverishment is 6, 4,
and 0.5 percent, for MOH, Régimen Subsidiado, and the Régimen
Contributivo respectively.

In Chile, the evidence of differing performance is also significant.
Figure 4.2 shows most of the newly poor due to health shocks come
from the private health insurance organizations (Instituciones de Salud
Previsional [ISAPREs]), participating as providers of mandatory health
insurance. In fact, figure 4.4 shows that while 4.5 percent and 7 percent
of households in the second and third quintiles, respectively, covered by
ISAPREs were impoverished by a health shock, this happened to only
1.5 percent and 2.5 percent of the same quintile populations covered by
the national health insurance Fondo Nacional de Salud (FONASA)
largely tax funded. Not surprisingly, people in the second and third
quintiles were the most vulnerable. The vast majority of those in the first

*Figure 4.4* Impoverishment Due to Health Shock,
by Household Income and Risk-Pooling
Mechanism, Chile, 2000 (percent)

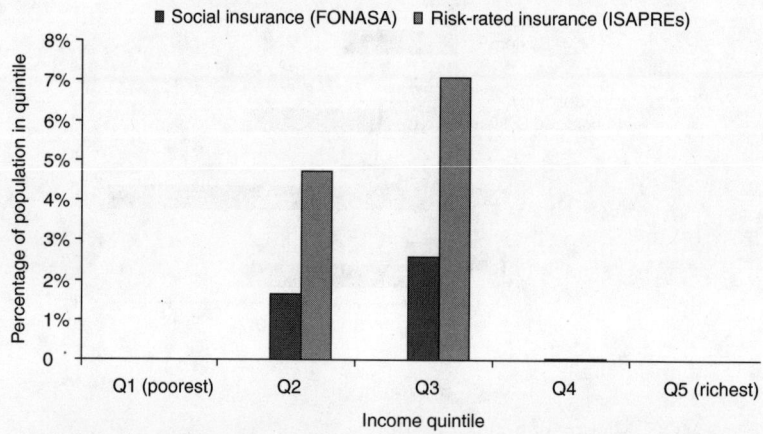

Q=Quintile.
*Note:* In Chile, households covered by private health insurance are more
likely to be impoverished in the wake of a health shock than those covered by
FONASA.
*Source:* Bitran et al. 2004.

quintile are already poor, and those in the fourth and fifth quintiles are
either better protected by the risk-pooling scheme in which they participate or their disposable income buffers the effects of health shocks.

## What Makes the Difference?

Why does the Régimen Subsidiado in Colombia perform better than the
traditional MOH? Why does FONASA do better on preventing poverty
than ISAPREs in Chile? In this section we discuss possible determinants
of performance emerging from the country cases and from the international literature on risk pooling and health insurance.

### Determinants of Performance

Health systems are complex living systems. Their performance is determined by governance, regulatory, and financial arrangements; by a multiplicity of inputs (for example, human resources, supplies, infrastructure,

*Figure 4.5* What Determines Health System Performance?

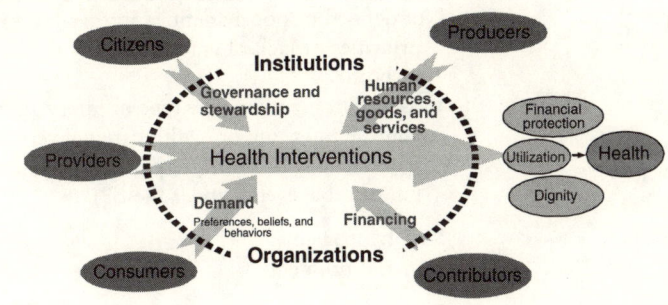

*Source:* Baeza 2002.

and equipment); and by demand patterns, all functioning within complex institutional and organizational settings (figure 4.5).

Similarly to health systems as a whole, the performance of risk-pooling organizations depends on multiple determinants. In LAC countries, causality cannot be determined from the type and amount of available data. Little research has been done on health system performance and its determinants in the region. The findings in the studies conducted for this report are preliminary; more in-depth evaluation needs to be completed.

## Characteristics of Risk-Pooling Systems

However, in line with international literature on determinants of risk-pooling performance, at least four key characteristic of the risk-pooling system seem to have an impact on performance in meeting health status and financial protection goals: the characteristics of the BP; the extent of strategic purchasing by the risk-pooling organization (the effectiveness of the purchaser-provider compact); the size of the pool; and the level and availability of equity subsidies. Other variables such as the extent of risk-pool fragmentation and the regulatory framework for risk-pooling organizations also play an important role. Table 4.1 summarizes the main determinants of performance.

*Benefits package.* The BP is of key importance in determining the performance of a risk-pooling arrangement. It defines a participant's entitlement to use a specified package of health care services under a set of conditions (for example, quality, waiting time, service price at delivery). These definitions largely determine the effectiveness of the risk-pooling scheme in ensuring access to health services with financial

*Table 4.1* Possible Determinants of the Performance of
Risk-Pooling Arrangements in Latin America

| | |
|---|---|
| BP problems | Not defined or poorly defined intervention priorities or lack of enforcement of the BP, or both |
| | Incongruities between the type of intervention and the financing or health care delivery mechanisms, or both (for example, including uninsurable events under the BP) |
| Utilization | Supply problems |
| | Demand problems |
| Organization and functional arrangements in the scheme | Problems with cross-subsidization from low-risk individuals to high-risk individuals (risk pooling) |
| | Problems with cross-subsidization from high-income groups to lower-income groups (equity subsidy) |
| | Problems in the relationship between purchaser and provider (strategic purchasing) |

*Source:* Baeza, Montenegro, and Núñez 2002.

protection. A BP with too many constraints and limitations, one with too few interventions, or one with the wrong interventions (for example, uninsurable events) will not work.

Alternative risk-pooling arrangements in the LAC region have traditionally shown significant differences with regard to the BP. Experience there suggests that a clear and explicit BP is important regardless of a country's predominant risk-pooling arrangement. Most national health service arrangements do not have explicit BPs. In LAC, most countries' constitutions specifically provide for every citizen's right to health or health care and the state's responsibility to ensure these rights (see chapter 6).

However, governments usually approach national health service arrangements and social insurance arrangements differently. While the regulatory framework for the health service determines that the BP is implicit and often covers everything, the regulatory framework for social insurance arrangements usually mandates an explicit BP. This distinction is becoming increasingly blurred in Latin America. Countries like Colombia (since 1994); Chile (since 1996 and particularly since the Plan de Acceso Universal con Garantias Explicitas [AUGE] reform in 2003); Mexico (2003); and Argentina (2003) are introducing explicit BPs for the population financed mostly out of fiscal subsidies.

The definition of a BP has to specify the health services included in the package. It should also contain clear guidelines and provisions for guaranteeing the conditions under which the covered services will be provided, including those pertaining to financial protection and dignity. A BP must therefore include the following elements:

- The list of health interventions (health care services), making sure that those services are indeed insurable events
- The acceptable service quality (clear definitions of the interventions and the eligibility of accredited providers)
- The appropriate timing for delivery of the health care services (maximum waiting times)
- Copayments, deductibles (if any), and stop-loss provisions
- Specific definitions on confidentiality, accommodations, privacy, access to patient information, patient rights, and other elements essential to the preservation of dignity.

*Strategic purchasing.* Drawing up the BP is only the first part of the challenge. Risk-pooling organizations need a mandate and the capacity to create the right incentive framework for health care providers to deliver the services defined in the BP and to monitor, verify, and enforce the BP conditions. Risk-pooling organizations do this mostly through strategic purchasing.

Strategic purchasing is the way most risk-pooling organizations (purchasers) use collected and pooled financial resources to buy health care services for their members. In the practical, day-to-day interaction between purchasers and providers, the purchaser, within a regulatory framework, plays a key role in defining a substantial part of the external incentives for providers to develop the appropriate provider-user interaction and health service delivery models. The purchaser is also responsible for continually monitoring and evaluating the quality and timing of the services provided for its insured. However, there is a difference between "strategic" purchasers and "passive" purchasers. A strategic purchaser continuously and actively responds to the following questions with new mechanisms and innovations: How should health services be purchased most efficiently for the covered population? What level of service quality must be assured? From whom should these services be purchased? How should these services be paid for? How should the delivery of health care services be monitored and supervised to guarantee they meet the specified conditions? How is the organization doing in terms of its impact on access to services and financial protection? (Preker and Langenbrunner 2005).

To achieve its mission and respond to these questions, a strategic purchaser needs freedom and a flexible management and regulatory framework, focused on the interests of the people it serves. For that, society needs to determine—through regulation but especially through sound governance arrangements—the right incentives to make the purchaser proactive and efficient in addressing these questions.

A strategic purchaser should be able to select the services and providers best suited to deliver the BP services and goods to its members. The strategic purchaser can therefore choose the specific conditions of a virtual or actual contract with providers regarding the payment mechanisms and price negotiations. In contrast, a passive purchaser does not have this freedom and can only develop a budget, often based on a historic trend or implemented as line-item budgets or both.

*Equity subsidies.* Insufficient equity subsidies are an evident problem in low-income countries in the LAC region. Lack of resources explains most of the problem, but inefficient management of collected funds also contributes to inadequacy. Protecting people in low-income countries, particularly the poor and indigent, is an urgent but complex task. These problems arise in a context of poverty and institutional and organizational instability that inhibit adequate generation and collection of funds for an equity subsidy.

Even with significant equity subsidies (the situation of many middle-income countries in the region), where public expenditures on health are substantial, deficiencies in the allocation of such subsidies can add up to poor performance. This happens in systems that do not provide enough effective cross-subsidization mechanisms from high- to low-income populations among different risk-pooling mechanisms or organizations. It also happens in many middle-income countries where subnational allocation of public subsidies is glaringly inequitable. In countries with federal governments with decreasing administrative power over subnational governments, fragmentation of financial protection might also occur. This happens in countries where decentralization of the federal structure fragments the risk pool (for example, Argentina and Mexico) and eventually leads to inequalities in regional allocations of equity subsidies. Historical budgets perpetuate regional differences. This problem is of utmost concern in public policy in health not only because of the consequences of an inequitable allocation of fiscal resources, but also because public policies perpetuate this inequity.

The other cause of potentially bad equity-subsidy performance of risk-pooling organizations is inefficient management or mechanisms for allocating the subsidy. A major distortion in the efficiency of allocating an equity subsidy is its lack of portability, meaning that equity subsidies do not follow individuals changing from one risk pool to another (Baeza and Copetta 1999). Because there is no mechanism for compensation, a covered individual or family may lose the subsidy just for changing jobs (see chapter 5). Demand-side subsidization is often mentioned as a solution for this problem. However, we use the term portability to denote that we do not see demand-side subsidization as a solution for insurance in general, but only for a particular form of demand-side subsidization in which the subsidy is directly linked to a specific BP.

## Insights from Colombia and Chile

What might explain the difference in performance in the case of Régimen Subsidiado in Colombia and FONASA in Chile? Data and methodological shortcomings make it difficult to be certain. However, the difference seems to be explained by a combination of BP, strategic purchasing, and portable public subsidies. Colombia's Régimen Subsidiado has a well-defined BP, portable public subsidies, and aggressive strategic purchasing by risk-pooling organizations. Paradoxically, the difference is not in the revenue-collection mechanism (which usually and erroneously is used to distinguish true Bismarck-type insurance from the rest). Both the Régimen Subsidiado and the national health fund (FONSASA) in Chile are financed mostly from general tax revenue rather than from contributions.

In the case of Chile, the same three determinants also seem to explain the difference. Chile did not define an explicit BP for the entire population until 2003. During the previous eight years, (FONASA) and the ISAPREs had significant differences in the composition of the BP, particularly for people in the lowest income distribution of the ISAPRE population (the contestable segment between the two risk-pooling schemes). Prior to the definition of the BP in Chile, the private ISAPRE packages covered many uninsurable events (or at least more frequent and less costly interventions) and included provisions for exclusions, preexisting conditions, and significant deductibles. FONASA increasingly concentrated on impoverishing insurable events such as childhood cancer, chronic renal failure, including transplants, and other such conditions. This difference is compounded by the lack of portability for public subsidies. Households in ISAPREs facing an impoverishing event requiring equity cross-subsidization were either forced to leave their –ISAPRE and go to FONASA or incur a significant income loss, and a significant proportion of those in the second and third quintiles fell into poverty as a result. The absence of an explicit package makes it technically difficult and inequitable to move toward portable public subsidies. Also, for most of the 1990s, FONASA and ISAPREs had significant differences in strategic purchasing of services related to catastrophic events.

In 1996, FONASA introduced contracting and demand-side and payment mechanisms similar to Diagnostic Related Groups (a risk-sharing mechanism) for costly complex health interventions. ISAPREs used fee-for-service payment mechanisms for too long. Only recently have they introduced more risk-sharing types of payment mechanisms (mostly since 2000, when they created additional catastrophe insurance).

Experience in LAC, described above, suggests that no matter what specific risk-pooling arrangement policy makers choose, success in improving health status and financial protection for the population may depend entirely on how key health financing functions (strategic purchasing, existence of explicit, aligned BP, and provider payment mechanisms) are implemented. Policy makers in LAC need to focus less on disputes over whether the Bismarck or the Beveridge model should be the reform choice and much more on how these financing functions are working to improve health status and financial protection. Besides potential inconsistencies with a well-functioning labor market and the difficulties it faces to extend risk pooling to the informal sector of the Bismarck model as we discuss in chapter 5, there are examples of well-functioning schemes under both types of arrangement.

# 5

# Risk Pooling for Everyone: The Challenges Posed by a Growing Informal Economy

TO PROTECT VULNERABLE HOUSEHOLDS from the impoverishing consequences of health shocks, participation in effective health risk–pooling arrangements must be broadened. To do this, policy makers in Latin America and the Caribbean (LAC) face significant challenges for three populations: the poor, the high-risk, and the self-employed and informal workers. The large and growing number of informal and unsalaried workers in LAC countries, a significant overlap in the incidence of informal employment and poverty, and high out-of-pocket expenditure on health make the inclusion of the informal and unsalaried sectors in risk-pooling arrangements one of the highest priorities in public health policy in the region today. In this chapter, we give close attention to this segment of the population.

This chapter is organized in three sections. The first section examines the challenge of extending risk-pooling to the nonparticipant population in general. The second section examines the incentives for households not to participate in contributory risk pooling. These include access to free publicly financed services and the perceived contribution-benefits gap set by design by the use of payroll tax as the predominant revenue collection mechanism for social insurance (SI). The last section explores options for increasing participation in contributory risk pooling by the informal and self-employed nonpoor, including eliminating or reducing the gap between contribution cost and perceived benefits.

## The Challenge of Extending Risk Pooling

As discussed in preceding chapters, the magnitude of out-of-pocket health expenditures in the region makes it clear that LAC needs to increase its people's participation in risk-pooling schemes (coverage). Diverse population segments either do not participate in risk-pooling schemes or do it only marginally as shown by very high levels of out-of-pocket expenditures. As shown in figure 5.1, three population groups can be differentiated by their capacity to contribute (broken line, see figure 1.1 for discussion):

• Individuals whose contribution capacity is above the average cost of the health benefits package (solid line) for their entire life cycle (the non-poor population)
• Individuals whose contribution capacity never reaches the average cost of the package at any time in their life cycle (the poor)
• Individuals whose contribution was above the average cost of the package for much of their lives but who reach an age (or health risk) for which the average cost of the package outstrips their capacity to contribute (high risk).

These distinctions are less relevant when risk pooling is organized as a single pool and with substantial or full financing from general taxation (for example, as in national health services or NHS systems). In these systems, financing of the risk pool occurs at the societal level, and every member of society, at least in theory, has access to the same package of services independent of their contributions. Under these systems, fiscal sustainability is the challenge, which explains why many countries have no option but a mixed system combining NHS and contributory risk-pooling arrangements.

Distinguishing among these three populations becomes essential for health policy formulation in countries where governments choose (or where fiscal constraints leave them no other option) to organize risk pooling through contributory health insurance (social or private) or through a combination of contributory and noncontributory systems. Most LAC countries have chosen the mixed system.

Different challenges are connected with extending risk pooling to each of these three populations in a contributory risk-pooling context. Neither the poor nor the high-risk populations (as defined in figure 5.1) can contribute without deepening their poverty. However, the strategies for each group are different. While the poor could not contribute at any time in their life cycle, the high-risk population, particularly the elderly, did contribute for much of their lives. Thus, most of the policy challenges regarding inclusion of the poor in risk pooling are related to public subsidy policy, particularly efficiency and targeting (see chapter 6 for a discussion of efficiency-enhancing public sector reforms). In contrast, the policy issues regarding the high-risk population are closely related to those of old-age income security policy, including

*Figure 5.1* Distinctive Populations by Capacity to Contribute

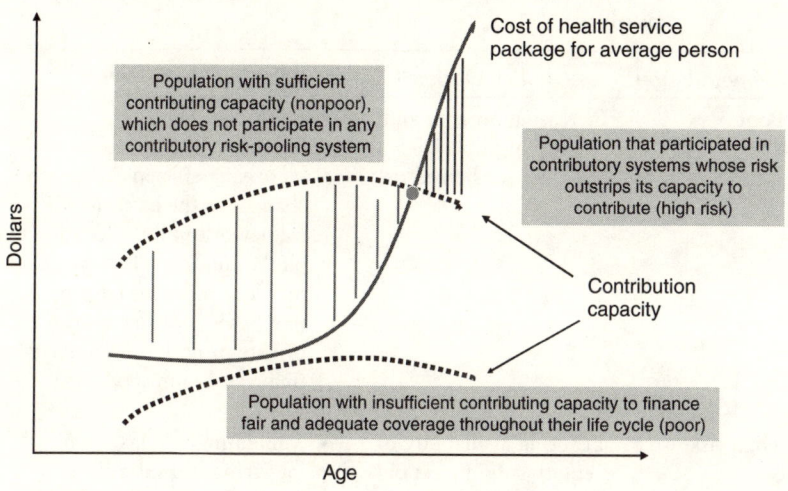

*Source*: Authors.

pensions. The challenges regarding these two populations, particularly how to include the poor, also differ significantly among countries in the LAC region. While publicly subsidized risk-pooling coverage is required for only 20 percent of the population in Chile, it is required for more than 63 percent of the population in Bolivia and 50 percent in Honduras.[1]

## Policy Options for Extending Risk Pooling

Extending participation in risk pooling in LAC is essential. What options do policy makers have to achieve this objective?

From figure 5.1 and the discussion above, it is clear that the options differ significantly according to the three subpopulations' capacity to pay. Table 5.1. summarizes the options for each of these groups. Although important reforms are under way in the region (see chapter 6) and there is a significant body of conceptual and technical work on what works and what does not to extend risk pooling, hard evidence and evaluations of the different policy options and instruments are still in a preliminary stage. We offer a discussion of these options as a way of catalyzing discussion and motivating further policy research in this

*Table 5.1* Major Policy Options for Extending Risk Pooling in
Latin America and the Caribbean in a Mixed Health
System (with contributory and noncontributory risk
pooling)

| Subpopulation | Policy Option | Possible Instruments |
|---|---|---|
| **Poor** | Increasing breadth and depth[a] of publicly pooling subsidized risk | • Additional fiscal resources, and/or <br> • Increasing efficiency through changes in the incentive framework in the allocation of public subsidies (for example, provider-payment reform; purchaser-provider split; private provision of publicly financed health services) |
| **High risk** | Ensuring availability of equity subsidies at old-age/high-risk stage | • Mandating savings (own intertemporal subsidies) <br> • Regulating contributory risk pooling in a way that ensures either intrapool or interpool subsidization[b] <br> • Public (societal-level) subsidies |
| **Nonpoor** | Eliminate barriers for participation in contributory risk pooling | • Facilitate supply of contributory health insurance <br> • Facilitate (through regulation) participation of self-employed and informal sector in contributory health insurance |
|  | Improving incentives for participation in contributory risk pooling, particularly for the informal and unsalaried nonpoor | • Improve enforcement of mandatory participation and evasion control <br> • Increase means testing for access to free, publicly subsidized health services <br> • Reduce the contribution-benefits gap[c] |

a. See discussion in chapter 1.
b. See discussion about alternative ways for financing equity subsidies in chapter 1.
c. See table 5.2.
*Source:* Authors.

area, but not as proven prescriptions for extending risk pooling in the region.

The challenges regarding the nonpoor population are also significant. This is the population served by mandatory SI schemes in most LAC countries, many of them with high participation levels (for example Mexico, Colombia, and Chile). However, part of this nonpoor population does not participate in contributory risk pooling and spends much more out-of-pocket than people who do participate. Why? What can policy makers in the region do to reduce this problem? The rest of this chapter focuses on potential causes and possible policy actions to overcome this problem in LAC.

## What Explains the Low Participation of the Informal Nonpoor in Contributory Risk-Pooling Schemes?

The informal nonpoor do not participate in contributory risk pooling for two main reasons. First, there may be barriers to their participation such as lack of insurance schemes (supply) and prohibitions or restrictions on participation (for example, for self-employed and unsalaried workers). Second, there is a conscious decision by households not to participate in contributory insurance derived from the national incentive framework.

### Barriers to Participation

Lack of supply of contributory risk pooling is not likely a significant cause of nonparticipation by the informal nonpoor in LAC. Almost every LAC country has a long and substantive tradition of social health insurance. In addition, the supply of voluntary private health insurance has been growing, particularly in the middle-income countries.

The focus of traditional Bismarck-type[2] SI on only formal salaried workers was, and in a few countries still is, a barrier to participation in contributory risk-pooling schemes for many self-employed and informal nonpoor workers. For many years, participation in SI organizations was mandatory for (and open only to) formal salaried workers. This left the rest of the nonpoor workers with no chance to participate. However, most countries in the region (for example, Argentina, Chile, Colombia, Ecuador, and Mexico) have identified this problem and have introduced laws and regulations to open participation in social security coverage (on a voluntary or mandatory basis) to unsalaried workers and, in some cases, even to informal workers. Colombia has introduced legislation regarding the base income for determining SI contributions by informal workers associated with cooperatives and will soon introduce administrative improvements in data collection and database cross-checking that would improve evasion monitoring.

Most of these innovations are recent in LAC. Those that have been in place longer show mixed results, depending on the specific benefits package (BP) being offered and the contribution cost. Despite this opening of SI, many informal and unsalaried workers still do not participate in the schemes. Why not?

## Holes in the Incentives Framework

Nonpoor households refrain from participating in a country's contributory risk pooling mainly because of holes in the incentive framework. Three factors shape their decision: their free access to noncontributory risk-pooling arrangements, specifically, free health services of acceptable quality from national health services (NHSs), which coexist with contributory SI in almost all LAC countries; their perception of a gap between the contribution cost and the benefits of participation (contribution-benefits gap); and their assessment of the costs and benefits of labor formalization, particularly in countries where participation in SI is closely linked to compliance with labor and tax laws.

*Incentives set by access to free, quality health services.* Access to free, quality health services may invite nonparticipation of nonpoor households in contributory risk-pooling schemes. If nonpoor households have access to fully subsidized services that satisfy them for free, they may decide not to buy in to contributory schemes. Again, except for potential fiscal unsustainability, this is not a problem for countries that have chosen to organize risk pooling through a single-pool, general tax–financed system open to all members of society. However, for mixed systems, it might constitute a significant problem if participation in contributory risk pooling is voluntary (or if the capacity to enforce mandatory participation is weak) and access to free NHSs is not means tested.

For some countries in the LAC region, this is indeed a problem. In Chile in 2002, Fondo Nacional de Salud (FONASA), the national health fund, discovered that many (about 300,000) nonpoor informal and self-employed workers using the free high-complexity services made no contribution at all or far lower contributions than legally expected. These findings suggest that if equity subsidization is to be provided through NHSs in a mixed system,[3] it is essential to ensure that access to free NHSs is targeted to the poor and to the high-risk population. Although access to quality, free health services is an incentive to nonparticipation in contributory risk pooling, if NHS covered all or most of this population's expected needs, we would not expect the exceedingly high out-of-pocket expenditures we observe today (which in practice mean nonparticipation). We know that NHSs do not provide such coverage. Why, then, do these households not participate in contributory risk pooling?

*The contribution-benefits gap.* In most LAC countries, workers are mandated to participate in contributory risk pooling, mainly in SI, through social security organizations. For most SI organizations in LAC, the payroll tax is the main source of revenue. The reliance of SI on the workplace and payroll taxes as the main revenue collection mechanism creates, by design, a gap between contributions and perceived benefits for most participants.

The rationale for relying on the payroll tax is to meet both the risk-sharing and the equity objectives of risk-pooling arrangements (described in chapter 4) with a single financing instrument. Indeed, the payroll tax contribution to SI was conceived as an instrument to ensure intrapool cross-subsidization. In other words, it was designed to ensure that people with the highest salaries contribute more (in absolute terms) than those with the lowest salaries. Since all participants enjoy the same BP, at least in theory, the payroll tax ensures that an actuarial surplus from lower-risk, higher-income individuals is generated to finance the actuarial deficits generated by higher-risk, lower-income individuals. Figure 5.2 illustrates this arrangement.

As shown in figure 5.2, the critical feature in SI is that the actuarial surplus (represented in area B of the figure) will be used to finance subsidies

*Figure 5.2* Cross-Subsidies in Traditional Social Insurance for Health

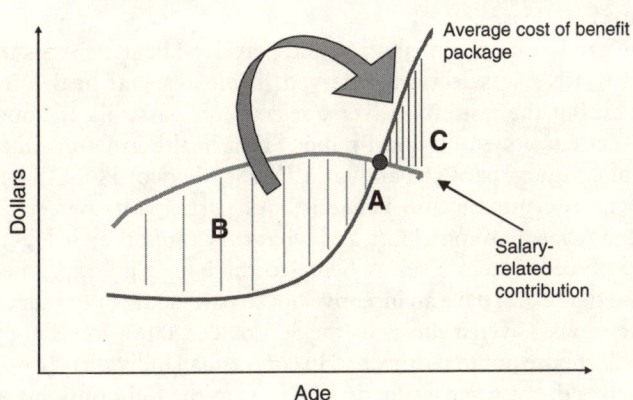

*Source:* Baeza 2000.

needed by lower-income, higher-risk groups (represented in area C). This feature can work well when all workers participate in a single SI scheme and under a regulatory framework or social contract that ensures that all members of the risk pool have access to the same package of health services when needed. However, in most Latin American countries, these critical prior assumptions and conditions are not fully realized for many reasons. Participation in SI is not universal due to the increasing proportion of informal and unsalaried workers, and neither the regulatory framework nor the social contract is strong enough to guarantee all participants equal access to the same health BP, even where such a package is explicitly guaranteed.

In addition, in the absence of a mandatory or guaranteed BP, contributions structured as a payroll tax constitute a mandate on minimum spending on health, rather than a definition of minimum consumption of insurance. Under this mandate structure, with a set, salary-linked contribution rate, SI providers have an incentive to reduce the gap via service *supply rationing* rather than by *risk rating* (that is, adjusting premium prices). At the same time, scheme participants have an incentive to close the gap by maximizing their use of services (or including as many services as possible in the BP they choose). That choice has no effect on their required contribution in a supply-rationed system, but it would eventually raise their contribution in a risk-rated system. Indeed, the primary distinction between SI and purely private, actuarially risk-rated health insurance is that SI providers cannot differentiate contributions by the groups they cover. However, like private health insurance providers, they still face incentives determined by known losses when covering low-income, high-risk participants, and often adjust their service provision to avoid or recoup these losses.

The gap between contribution and perceived benefits feeds the incentives for adverse selection observed in most social health insurance schemes. But the resulting adverse selection is particularly important in voluntary enrollment in quasi-public SI for health in Latin America (for example, Seguro para la Familia in IMSS, Mexico; FONASA in Chile; and Seguro Campesino in Ecuador). All participants perceiving a gap between what they contribute and what they think they will get (that is, if they perceive themselves as being to the left of point A, the subsidy point in figure 5.2) have an incentive not to participate or to reduce (evade) contributions. Given a choice by the SI provider, if evasion is not possible, they will choose not to participate. In contrast, all individuals who perceive themselves in the reverse situation (that is, to the right of point A) would actively seek enrollment and would be among the first to sign up, if given the option. This is the main reason for the adverse selection observed when enrollment in social health insurance is made voluntary.

The gap (and resulting disincentives) is increased for low-risk, high-income participants when access is difficult or health service quality is low, or both. The effect is to reduce the perceived benefits of participation. The same effect occurs when services are added to the BP that participants perceive they would not use at all (for example, normal delivery for a couple that has decided not to have children), or when health insurance is bundled with other SI benefits that many individuals believe they are unlikely to receive. The effect in this case is to add costs to the package with no perceived increase in benefits.

For example, the bundled mandated contribution to old-age income pensions might simply be perceived as an additional cost or tax that increases the contribution-benefits gap if workers perceive that it is unlikely that they will ever get a benefit from their contributions. Indeed, in many LAC countries, given their relatively short life expectancy, low-income workers are unlikely to receive pension benefits and, in fact, may place a low value on these benefits. Other individuals may have chosen to substitute mandatory systems for alternative forms of saving and investment to cover the bulk of their financial needs in old age. There is ample evidence (James 1999; Arenas De Mesa 2000; Holzmann, Packard, and Cuesta 2000; Gill, Packard, and Yermo 2004) that the likelihood of receiving pension benefits is low for the self-employed, lower-income workers, workers who take formal jobs sporadically, and even for workers with large gaps in their contribution histories (for example, due to long periods of unemployment). In these circumstances, bundling health coverage with retirement pensions—and the resulting increase in the gap between contribution and benefits—may not only contribute to adverse selection and low demand for health insurance, but may also contribute to the wide array of incentives for individuals to enter self-employment or unregulated employment.

The gap between contribution and perceived benefits creates incentives for nonparticipation for part of the nonpoor population. But, does this matter, since participation in SI is mandatory for nonpoor workers? It matters a great deal. SI plays a significant role in providing a large part of the population with health coverage, particularly in middle-income countries where coverage well exceeds 40 percent of the total population (for example, Argentina, Chile, Costa Rica, and Mexico). In most LAC countries, however, household participation (even of the nonpoor) in SI schemes is still limited. Why?

Households make decisions about whether to participate in social health insurance. Moreover, the structure of SI, and the wider social protection system may be a contributing factor in a household decision about leaving the formal labor market altogether. Although economic and labor regulations, working conditions, and preferences for flexibility or for entrepreneurship play a major role in these decisions (Maloney 2004), the perception among nonpoor contributing workers that they receive less in benefits than they pay in contributions (the contribution-benefits gap) can also be an important factor in the decision to enter self-employment or un-regulated forms of employment. Although debate is increasing about how much the rising cost of SI contributes to informality (Maloney 2004), there is still less definitive evidence about the magnitude of this incentive and the relative importance of the contribution-benefits gap than about other labor regulation incentives. Still, anecdotal evidence increasingly suggests that this gap plays an important role.

These days, mainly for practical reasons, enforcing the mandate for nonpoor workers to participate in payroll tax–financed SI is largely restricted to formal salaried workers for four reasons. First, by histor-ical design, SI focuses on formal workers and their families and be-cause its contribution-collection mechanism is structured as a payroll tax deduction, only firms and workers in compliance with the labor code are covered. Second, due to the difficulty of correctly assessing employment status and household income (*unobservability*), the par-ticipation of informal and unsalaried workers in SI is essentially voluntary. Third, the gap between contribution and perceived benefits is relevant for a significant proportion of the nonpoor population, cre-ating strong incentives for adverse selection. Fourth, bundling health coverage with other less desirable benefits in most social protection systems often creates an extra cost without adding to perceived bene-fits, increasing incentives for adverse selection.

Given the practical limitations of enforcing mandatory participation in SI and the predominance of payroll tax–financed SI as a contributory risk-pooling mechanism in the region, informality in LAC makes it difficult to extend contributory risk pooling even to the nonpoor. This relatively low participation in itself would not be problematic over time if the trend in formalization were incremental, which would allow for increasing enforcement capacity of mandatory participation in SI. This was the case in most member countries of the Organisation for Economic Co-operation and Development (OECD) that opted for the Bismarck SI model and which have now achieved all but universal coverage. The current trend in LAC is also unlike the experience of OECD and other countries that have achieved universal coverage such as Korea and Taiwan. Growing informality (figure 5.3) poses an enormous challenge to Latin American countries in achieving universal risk-pooling coverage.

In this context, although all organizational arrangements for risk pooling have limitations in reaching the informal poor, traditional SI exhibits the most significant limitations.

*Cost of labor formalization.* From the preceding sections, informal labor clearly poses a challenge to the extension of contributory risk pooling,

*Figure 5.3* Growth of Informal Sector in Latin America,
1990, 1995, and 2000
(percentage of nonagricultural employment)

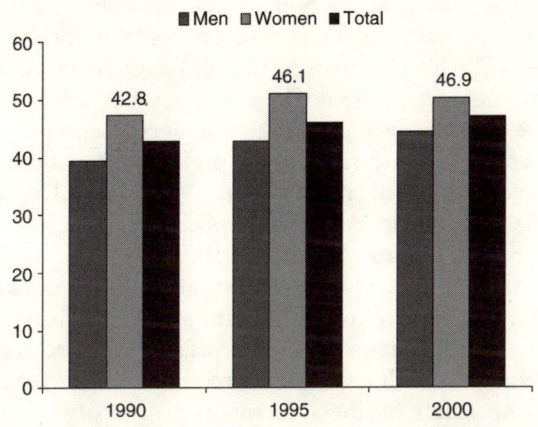

*Source:* ILO 2004.

particularly through payroll tax–financed SI. But, is the reverse also true? Does payroll tax–financed risk pooling in health pose a challenge to formalization of the labor force?

There is ample evidence that a significant proportion of households choose to go in and out of the formal labor market according to expected net income in one sector or another. Many individuals choose to work informally. Among informal workers, self-employment in particular is a status into which agents with a lower aversion to risk, a desire for independence, a greater endowment of entrepreneurial talent, or with all three motives are likely to self-select (Knight 1921; Laffont 1979). Empirical evidence from both developed (Taylor 1996; Uusitalo 1999; Guiso and Paiella 2000) and developing countries (Blau 1985; Vijverberg 1986; Yamada 1996; Maloney 1998a, 1998b, 2004) shows that labor regulations, economic conditions, and individual preferences play an important role in household decisions in this regard. Indeed, survey interviews of informally self-employed workers in Mexico (Maloney 2004) reveal that more than 58 percent of self-employed men left formal employment because they were not paid enough or sought greater independence. In Brazil, 65 percent of self-employed men and 41 percent of self-employed women say they would not want to take formal employment because they are happy with their current jobs. A similar portion of informal salaried workers in Brazil also report satisfaction with their unregulated, uncovered employment (Maloney 2004).

Although economic conditions and labor regulations play an important role in household decisions regarding participation in the formal labor market, an abundance of both theory and empirical evidence suggests that they also base this decision on the contribution-benefits gap in the structure of SI schemes, choosing to avoid payroll taxes altogether. As a consequence of the gap, should the value of a worker's nonwage benefits fall below the perceived cost, even risk-averse workers with no significant entrepreneurial aspirations may prefer to move into the informal sector and be compensated entirely in cash.[4] Torche and Wagner (1997) show that mandated benefits levy an implicit tax, especially on younger workers. In a panel of Latin American countries, Packard (2002a) finds that the size of the total payroll tax for social security lowers the number of contributors in the workforce.[5] Fiorito and Padrini (2001) arrive at similar results in an analysis of labor taxes in developed economies. In developing countries with less capacity to enforce labor regulations, the relatively large small business sector and diversity of unregulated employment opportunities allow workers to avoid mandated benefits and choose how they are compensated (Maloney 2000 and 2004).

Further, the individual's or household's decision to work formally or informally is not necessarily dichotomous. Under an SI scheme with a salary- or income-related contribution structure, and in the presence of weak enforcement of labor regulations and large gaps between contribution and benefits, workers can and do bargain with employers over formal wages and remuneration outside the formal contract. Ultimately, an individual's bargaining position with a prospective informal employer will depend on broader market elasticity of supply and demand. And many employers are likely to choose to evade participation without regard for what workers actually prefer. However, where the benefits gap is perceived as large, it is likely that workers will choose to be formally remunerated at the lowest level that allows them to qualify for benefits. In the case of SI for health, the benefits are the same for all participants in the SI scheme, regardless of their absolute contribution.

Similarly, self-employed workers would choose to report—and make contributions on—just enough income to qualify for benefits. Indeed, Valdes (2002) reports that administrators of Chile's FONASA (national health insurer) identified up to 500,000 workers who reported incomes and made contributions on the minimum salary that entitled them to health insurance coverage, despite their significantly higher earnings according to tax authorities. In Chile, the mandate to contribute is bundled for health insurance and pension coverage in the privately administered retirement income security system. Some self-employed workers based their contributions to the pension system on the legal minimum wage for benefits in FONASA. This behavior may have been driven by demand for health insurance coverage rather than by the desire for pension benefits, even when the pension system is based on individual savings accounts. Although other important factors play a role (for example, abuse of the legal protection within the system,[6] rigidities in the budget implementation system), a similar gap between contribution and perceived benefits may partly explain the significant contribution reduction observed for the Régimen Contributivo in the Colombian health system.

We close this section with a note of caution. Despite the large body of theoretical literature and empirical evidence showing the *negative* impact of high rates of payroll tax contributions and a large gap between contribution and perceived benefits on household incentives to participate in SI, the payroll tax is but one of myriad factors that add to the cost of formalization for workers and prospective employers. SI for health risks and the wider social protection system is embedded deeply within the regulatory framework of a country's product and factor markets. In many countries, the decision to insure cannot be divorced from the decision to comply with regulations and taxation that have nothing to do with covering the risks to household welfare from health shocks or other adverse events.

Furthermore, while there are empirical estimates of the negative impact of high payroll contributions, evidence of a positive reaction to lowering contribution rates is still scarce. Rofman (2003) shows that, despite the introduction of individual retirement accounts and a substantial cut in employer contribution rates for SI in Argentina, participation in the social security system fell dramatically throughout the 1990s. Gill, Packard, and Yermo (2004) point out that worker participation is still unacceptably low across Latin America despite the lower labor-market distortions brought about by the shift to individual accounts in the part of the SI system that covers income losses from old age. Thus, narrowing the gap between contribution and households' perceived benefits from SI might be a necessary but far from sufficient condition to increase the incentives to participate both in contributory risk pooling and in the formal labor sector.

## Policy Options for Extending Contributory Risk Pooling among the Informal and the Self-Employed Nonpoor

Considering the growing employment informality, the mixed nature of most health systems in LAC, and the lack of conceptual and empirical developments on how to address the problem, extending risk pooling among the informal nonpoor is one of the most challenging and complex priorities for policy makers in the region. This section reviews some of the main options in line with the discussion and findings above and in earlier chapters.

As discussed above, the most important challenge in terms of predominant models of contributory health insurance in LAC is that participation in contributory risk pooling is essentially voluntary for informal and unsalaried workers. Given the workplace and salary-related nature of SI as well as the unobservability of informal workers' employment and income, enforcing a mandate for participation in contributory schemes is almost impossible. This means that more important than the mandate is the need to find other incentives (or eliminate disincentives) for the informal nonpoor to place greater value on participating in voluntary contributory risk pooling.

A distinction must be made between informal and unsalaried workers. Neither is typically subject to payroll tax contributions and both pay consumption taxes such as the value added tax (VAT). But, while informal workers do not pay any kind of income tax and are usually totally outside the formal tax systems in the economy (except for paying consumption taxes), unsalaried workers do pay forms of income tax (for example, a self-employed lawyer who pays taxes based on billings). However, unsalaried workers are usually not mandated to contribute to SI because they receive no salary, have no employer, and are not usually associated with a specific workplace.[7] For practical enforcement purposes at this time, the difference is minor but it might become important once the income observability problem is technologically solved for unsalaried workers. FONASA in Chile has experimented with internal revenue service consumption/income databases in this direction. However, for most countries in the region, enforcing mandatory participation of informal and unsalaried workers in health insurance will remain unfeasible for a long time.

Policy makers have at least four nonmutually exclusive options: facilitate (through regulation) participation of self-employed and informal workers in contributory health insurance; improve enforcement of mandatory participation and evasion control; increase means testing for access to free publicly subsidized health services; or reduce the contribution-benefits gap. The first two are self-explanatory.

Increasing means-tested access to free publicly subsidized health services is important to reduce incentives for nonparticipation among the informal nonpoor and to target scarce fiscal resources on the poor. Coexistence of most subsidized national health services and contributory health insurance provides nonpoor informal households with multiple alternatives. This, added to difficult enforcement of mandatory participation and labor contracts, allows for high mobility between these two systems. If a country decides to make the nonpoor contribute for their risk pooling coverage, it is essential to ensure that means testing is used to determine access to subsidized health services.

Although reasonable doubts persist about the relative importance of the contribution-benefits gap to informality, there are few doubts that it contributes to evasion, undercontribution, and, most likely, refusal to participate in any way in contributory risk pooling. This is why it is so important for policy makers to explore ways of narrowing the contribution-benefits gap in each country's own evidence-based context.

The contribution-benefits gap can be reduced by delinking risk-pooling financing from labor status, fundamentally shifting away from the use of payroll taxes; reducing perceived costs (contribution) of participation in contributory risk pooling; and increasing the perceived benefits of participation. Table 5.2 summarizes some of the main policy options to reduce the contribution-benefits gap.

## Delinking Risk-Pool Financing from Labor Status

Delinking risk-pool financing from the labor status of individuals and their household dependents may thus be an important step for policy makers to reduce the gap between contribution and perceived benefits and increase incentives for informal and unsalaried workers to participate in contributory risk pooling. In practice, policy makers have two main means of replacing payroll taxes: general taxation and other revenue collection mechanisms that reduce the contribution-benefits gap, most likely risk-related premiums.

*Delinking with a shift toward general taxation financing.* General taxation is potentially the most efficient and also the most equitable financing mechanism for risk pooling, depending on the progressivity of tax collection instruments and subsequent public spending (Mossialos et al. 2002; Savedoff 2004). The primary benefit of financing health coverage through general tax revenues is that health risks are effectively pooled across the entire tax-paying population. A broader tax base means that contributions are spread over a larger share of the population than might otherwise be the case, particularly where employers and workers can evade payroll contributions. Shifting to general revenue financing can also be less regressive, if revenue from rents, capital gains, and profits are taxed. Of all the sources of financing, general taxation entails the lowest transaction costs for allocating equity subsidies for a given level of risk-pool fragmentation because the entire society becomes a single pool (Savedoff 2004). Moving to general taxation could also have a positive impact on formalization in the labor market and on labor mobility, although

Table 5.2 Policy Options for Reducing the Contribution-Benefits Gap for the Informal Nonpoor

| Strategy | Instruments | Challenges | Remedies |
|---|---|---|---|
| Delink risk-pool financing from labor market status and employment sector | Shift away from payroll tax financing toward general taxation or risk-rated premiums | Fiscal sustainability (general tax strategy) | Incremental delinking |
| | | Equity (risk-rated premium strategy) | Tax reform, use of VAT as main taxation instrument |
| | | Unobservability of employment status and income in largely informal labor markets | Proactive and explicit public equity subsidization |
| Mandate minimum consumption (coverage) rather than minimum spending | Move away from mandates that specify percent of payroll taxes for health coverage and define mandatory benefits package of mainly insurable events; mandate package as minimum universal coverage, provided by multiple or single insurers | Equity: part of the population might not be able to afford the minimum package | Incremental growth of the package |
| | | Political economy of explicit prioritization | Focus incremental general taxation financing on subsidizing the package first for those who cannot afford it |
| | | | Contain package cost (efficiency gains) |

Reduce perceived
costs (contribution)

Seek efficiency gains resulting
in service unit cost reduction
(for example, implementation
of strategic purchasing)

Regulate to create incentives for
large pools and aggregate
catastrophic events (risks) in a
single pool (truncation of
pyramid of risk)

Subsidize the cost of the
benefits package

Unbundle health insurance from
other "benefits" (for example,
pensions)

Reduce risk-pooling fragmentation
through at least "virtual pools"
(single rules, single BP, portability)

Political economy of
implementing purchaser-
provider split and strategic
purchasing

Fiscal sustainability

Incremental growth of
mandatory benefits package

*(Table continues on the following page.)*

Table 5.2 (continued)

| Strategy | Instruments | Challenges | Remedies |
|---|---|---|---|
| Increase perceived benefits | Increase access, quality, and responsiveness of service providers | Fiscal sustainability | Incremental implementation |
| | Bundle contributory risk pooling with desirable benefits (for example, burial insurance) | Political economy of introducing strategic purchasing | In multiple pool environment truncation of risk pyramid, basic risk-equalization in the allocation of public subsidies for benefits package, and strong consumer protection regulation. |
| | Concentrate benefits package on insurable events | Political economy of excluding uninsurable events from benefits package (for example, gender, public health) | |
| | Increase choice of service providers and insurance providers | "Cherry picking" behavior by insurers | |
| | Increase portability of public subsidies | Political economy of demand-side subsidization | |

*Source:* Authors.

consistent regulatory reforms in the wider economy would also be required to increase the benefits of formalizing for households and employers. Moving toward general tax–financed risk pooling requires that the mandate for a standard BP avoid inequities and inefficiency, especially during the transition.

Moving away from a payroll tax is not always welcomed by social security managers and is sometimes resisted by policy makers in health ministries. There are three main arguments against a shift to general tax–financing. First, the providers of public services in the health sector see in the payroll tax a more independent and secure revenue source that is safe from annual political budget discussions. Second, and related to the first point, the payroll tax is perceived to be less cyclical than general revenue sources in the sector. Third, payroll tax–financing makes it more difficult for governments to cut health services, because the contribution gives workers a sense of entitlement that they will defend and which creates a powerful political deterrent.

However, for many reasons, regular public debate on the amount a country decides to allocate to health, and public scrutiny on the way these funds are used, are highly desirable. Independent earmarked sources of revenue, such as a payroll tax, can give considerable autonomy to SI institutions and health ministries that can then limit the extent to which these institutions respond to public questioning of their performance and use of resources. Furthermore, although health allocations can come under pressure during economic downturns that lower governments' overall revenue, financing through payroll contributions and employment can have similar procyclical patterns—particularly employment in sectors that comply with the mandate to contribute. Finally, although payroll taxes do confer a strong sense of entitlement and a deterrent to cuts in services, in Latin America's context, this may often translate into capture by elites rather than protection of services, particularly for the poorest. A first-best entitlement that could create the same deterrent—desirable even purely on efficiency grounds—would be a clearly, explicitly defined BP, with fiscal contributions indexed to its costs.

All these issues are important for policy makers to consider when deciding whether to delink or not. However, the LAC region has many examples of budget and revenue control of payroll tax–financed SI organizations. In some cases payroll tax collection is conducted by a government-controlled organization, and it is subjected to budget planning and approval (for example, FONASA in Chile until the late 1990s, Instituto Nacional de Servicios Sociales para Jubilados y Pensionados [PAMI] in Argentina during the 1990s), which determines the same level of central government control as general tax transfers. In other cases, the government has not paid into the social security organization its corresponding payroll tax for public workers. On occasion, it has even mandated the social security organization to invest its reserves in long-term (often high-risk) government bonds. In these instances, revenue independence and security have been compromised. In many other cases, revenue independence and security are compromised for the benefit of SI. Many governments in the region heavily subsidize SI operational deficits, generating significant inequities in the allocation of public health subsidies (for example, Instituto Mexicano de Seguridad Social [IMSS] and Instituto de Seguridad y Servicios Sociales para los Trabajadores del Estado [ISSSTE] in Mexico). Thus, at first sight, ensuring independent and secure financing for risk pooling seems to depend more on governance arrangements than on the financing mechanism. Ensuring independence in financing is difficult when, for example, the president appoints SI chief executive officers, and there are no independent oversight and regulatory agencies. Research into SI governance is urgently needed in the region.

If delinking and general taxation offer so many advantages, why have LAC countries not already moved in this direction? Most OECD and many developing countries have already started to do so. Even countries with long traditions of Bismarck-type SI systems are moving toward general taxation to finance their risk-pooling systems (for example, France and Spain, box 5.1). In fact, countries that have opted for general revenue financing typically started with fragmented voluntary and then mandatory SI systems. Countries that already have strong Beveridge-type systems (for example, Sweden, United Kingdom, and New Zealand) are further strengthening this model. Even in Germany, recent proposals to reform segments of the welfare system aim at moving health finance toward general taxation.

Latin American countries, particularly middle-income countries, are already making significant efforts in fiscal financing of risk pooling (figure 5.4). However, although Latin America ranks first among developing-country regions in terms of general tax–funded health expenditures (about 3.2 percent of gross domestic product [GDP]), it is still below the OECD average of 4.0 percent (box 5.2).

Increasing general tax allocation to the health sector in Latin America to replace payroll tax–financing would be difficult in the short run. The tax collection capacity of countries in the region is among the lowest in the world, only slightly ahead of Asia-Pacific and Sub-Saharan Africa (table 5.3). It would also prove difficult without governance improvements in SI and SI-government relations and changes in the way fiscal subsidies are allocated in the sector (for example, in the absence of indexation of fiscal allocations and an explicit BP). In addition, many SI organizations might not welcome such a change, which could reduce their financial independence.

*Box 5.1* Spain's Shift from Bismarck to Beveridge:
         Delinking Risk-Pool Financing from Labor Status

As part of a broad process of change in the health sector and Spanish society in general, the health financing system in Spain underwent radical changes in the 1980s and 1990s. After the 1980s, Spain shifted from a social security scheme, financed by payroll taxes, to a national health service, financed by general taxation. Today, almost 100 percent of Spain's expenditures in health are public.

Spain's transition to democracy and the constitution approved by popular referendum in 1978 gave new impetus to health care sector reform. Important changes from this period that influenced later changes in health financing include the creation of a separate organization within the social security system to administer health care services and consolidate most health care programs and organizations under the umbrella of the Ministry of Health. This ministry was established as an independent entity in 1981.

The reform process culminated in 1986 in the passage of the General Health Care Act after nearly four years of public and parliamentary discussions. The act also provided a unified legal framework for many of the previous piecemeal reforms and called for a tax-based financing system. All the publicly managed health services were consolidated in a single national organization and a few other regional organizations (Cataluña and the Basque Country), within the framework of the newly decentralized organization of the state. The Spanish National Health System (SNHS) was subsequently devolved to the 17 autonomous communities that have fully managed their regional health services since 2001 under the direction of the SNHS.

Consistent with the reforms introduced by the General Health Care Act, the funding sources for the health care system were drastically modified in 1989. Beginning that year, new budgets were financed at 70 percent from general taxation and only 30 percent from payroll tax contributions.

In the mid 1990s, as a result of general negotiations and agreements (the *Pactos de Toledo*) signed by political parties and trade unions, it was agreed that all financing would come from general taxation and that individual contributions would be progressively phased out by 2000. In 1999, one year ahead of schedule, the entire health care budget in Spain came from general taxation. Today, Spanish regions receive health care funding as part of their general funding from the central government, proportionate to their population and the increase of fiscal revenues raised in the region with a few adjusting factors (population age, number of temporary residents, and services provided to the national system or to other regions).

Today, only workers' compensation for work-related injuries or diseases are financed via individual employer and employee contributions.

*Source:* Fernandez 2004.

*Figure 5.4* Composition of Health Financing in Latin America
and the Caribbean and OECD Countries, 2001

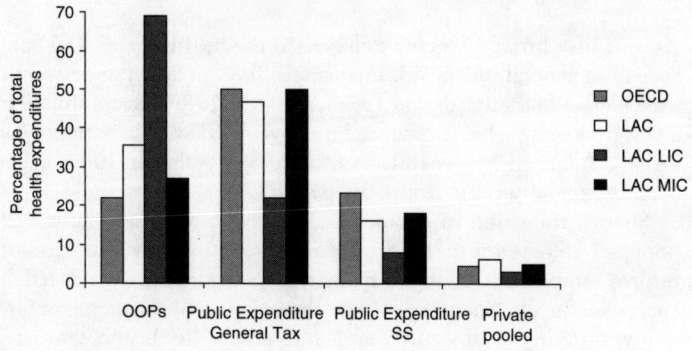

OECD=Organisation for Economic Co-operation and Development;
LAC=Latin America and Caribbean; LIC=lower-income countries; MIC=middle-
income countries; OOPs=out-of-pocket expenditures; SS=social security.
*Source*: Authors from OECD 2004 and WHO 2004 data.

*Table 5.3* Central Government Revenues, Early 2000s
          (percent of averages[a])

|  | Total Revenue as % of GDP | Tax Revenue as % of GDP | Payrol Tax as % of GDP |
|---|---|---|---|
| Americas[b] | 20.0 | 16.3 | 2.3 |
| Sub-Saharan Africa | 19.7 | 15.9 | 0.3 |
| Central Europe, Baltics, Russia, and other Former Soviet Republics | 26.7 | 23.4 | 8.1 |
| Middle East and North Africa | 26.2 | 17.1 | 0.8 |
| Asia and Pacific | 16.6 | 13.2 | 0.5 |
| Small islands (Pop. < 1 million) | 32.0 | 24.5 | 2.8 |
| Low-income countries | 17.7 | 14.5 | 0.7 |
| Low middle-income countries | 21.4 | 16.3 | 1.4 |
| Upper middle-income countries | 26.9 | 21.9 | 4.3 |
| High-income countries | 31.9 | 26.5 | 7.2 |

a. Unweighted averages
b. IMF regional and income categorizations
*Source:* Schieber et al. 2006.

*Box 5.2* Trends in Latin American and Caribbean Tax
           Policies: Balancing the Efficiency-Equity Tradeoff

Tax policies and systems vary greatly from country to country in the
LAC region, reflecting different sociopolitical histories, tax-collection
capacities, and reactions to changes in thinking about tax and development policy.

In the 1950s and 1960s, tax policy discussions in Latin America
reflected the "developmentalist" views common in the postwar era.
According to this view, the two main aims of taxation were to raise
revenue to finance the state as the "engine of development" and to
redistribute income and wealth. Most people thought both goals could
be achieved largely by imposing high effective tax rates on income. The
depressing effects of taxes on investment and saving were judged small.
It was even argued that high tax rates made it easier to lead private
investors by the visible hand of well-designed fiscal incentives into the
investment most needed for development. A highly progressive personal
income tax (with marginal rates up to 60 percent) buttressed by a
substantial corporate income tax (often between 40 and 50 percent) was
considered the ideal tax system. Consumption taxes—mainly of excise
taxes, customs duties, and cascading manufacturer sales taxes—were
grudgingly accepted as necessary for revenue purposes.

This line of thinking changed dramatically in the 1970s and 1980s.
Today, most economists and policy makers believe that high tax rates
not only discourage and distort economic activity but are also ineffective in redistributing income and wealth. Most specialists prefer a
broad-based consumption tax, with few exemptions, and selectively
higher tax rates for items that either carry negative externalities or are
considered "bads" by society, such as gasoline, tobacco, and alcohol.
Economists now argue that the income tax should be as broad as possible and treat all incomes as uniformly as possible.

Reflecting this new view, income tax rates on both people and cor-
porations were cut sharply from the 50 percent and 40 percent level on
personal and corporate income, respectively, to the 20 percent and 30
percent range throughout LAC. Taxes related to international trade
were also cut as a part of widely accepted liberalization policies. This
decline in income tax rates and trade tariffs was accompanied by an increase in the personal exemption rate and reductions in the income
bracket to which the top rates of taxation apply. VATs are now seen as
the mainstay of the revenue system in most countries in the region. VAT
rates rose on average from 10 percent when first introduced to about 15
percent in 2001. This combination of falling tariffs and income tax rates
and rising indirect taxes yielded modest increases in overall tax revenues
across the region. Between the 1970s and 2000, the unweighted average

(*Box continues on the following page.*)

*Box 5.2* (continued)

of aggregate tax effort rose by about two percentage points of GDP to 14 percent of national income. Taxes on goods and services (mostly VAT) were the main source of this increase, more than offsetting declines in taxes on personal income and on trade.

However, LAC countries still tax a much smaller share of output than do richer countries. In particular, when compared to richer countries, Latin American governments take a much lower share of tax from personal income. This is primarily due to the lower rates applied to personal than to corporate income. Governments in richer countries also collect far more in social security taxes, VAT, and sales taxes and much less in taxes on trade. Property taxes that are low in developed countries are even lower in Latin America. These differences can be partially explained by the higher incomes in developing countries that typically translate into higher government expenditure. However, with a few exceptions (namely, Nicaragua, Uruguay, and Brazil) most LAC tax efforts lie below the international average even in relation to incomes.

How then can government revenues be increased and taxes made more progressive in Latin America, without excessively compromising the gains in economic efficiency that have been attained over the last 30 years? Tax policy presents tradeoffs between equity and efficiency that cannot be ignored. There is no such thing as a free lunch, and any effort to make taxes more equitable will have efficiency costs. However, countries could follow some broad principles to make tax systems more effective and marginally more progressive at a relatively low cost to efficiency.

First, tax bases should be as broad as possible. Although a broad-based consumption tax will still discourage work effort, it will distort economic choices between goods and services less if everyone is taxed at the same rate. Second, tax rates should be as low as possible, provided that they raise sufficient revenue to finance appropriate government expenditure. The broader the tax base, the lower the tax rate needs to be to generate a given level of revenue. Third, indirect taxes can be more effective and are not always regressive. In particular, VATs (generally preferable to excise or import taxes) can be made less regressive by exempting a few key items consumed in greater quantities by lower-income households than by wealthier families. Fourth, there is room to improve personal income tax collections. Collections from personal income taxes are low in Latin America, even when compared with countries at the same income levels. Higher collections can be sought first by closing loopholes and enforcing compliance with existing rates; only after that should tax rates be raised, if still necessary. Finally, property taxes are currently underused and should be made to generate more revenue.

*Source:* de Ferranti, Perry, Ferreira, and Walton 2004.

*Figure 5.5* Taxes Collected Relative to Income per Capita in
Latin America and Selected Industrial Countries

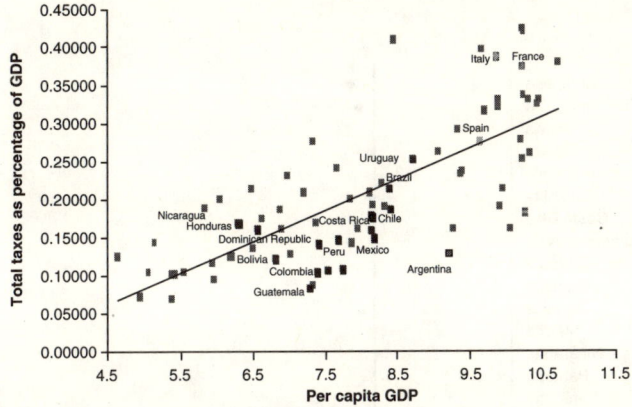

*Source*: World Bank staff using World Development Indicators Dataset of
2004.

This shift is unlikely to occur in the short run, considering LAC countries' lagging tax generation and collection performance (box 5.2 and figure 5.5).

The near future looks no better for LAC countries if recent trends in tax collection continue. Revenue performance over the past few decades has been disappointing, stagnant in some regions. Figure 5.6 shows the evolution of tax and nontax revenue for 22 countries in the region during the 1990s. The annual change in tax and nontax revenue as a percentage of GDP on average decreased in seven countries during the 1990s, and remained essentially constant (or grew less than 2 percent) in eight countries. Only in the seven remaining countries did tax collections and revenue grow faster.

Tax reforms also will not be easy in the LAC region for political reasons. The politics of such reforms has proven to be complex, and interest groups have proven adept at containing such reforms, even in countries where the tax base is obviously too low for what is expected at their current per capita GDP (for example, Mexico and Argentina).

Not every country is in the same situation. Countries with ratios of tax revenue to GDP above 20 percent (Chile, Panama, and Uruguay) or even 30 percent (Jamaica and St. Vincent) might be able to shift faster than countries such as Argentina, Colombia, and Mexico, which are below 15 percent.

*Figure 5.6* Annual Changes in Tax and Nontax Revenues in
          Selected Latin American and Caribbean Countries
          (percent of GDP)

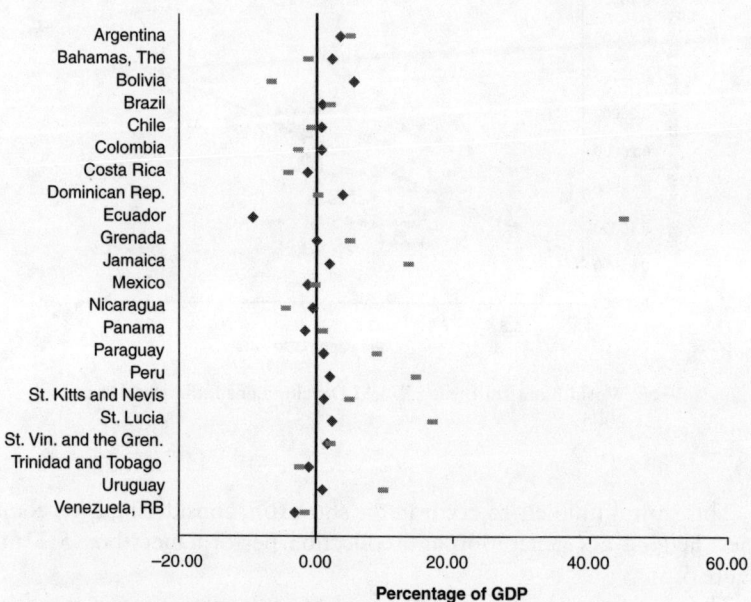

Square: Annual percentage change in nontax revenue as percentage of GDP.
Diamond: Annual percentage change in tax revenue as percentage of GDP.
*Source:* World Bank Staff using IMF data.

The low tax and nontax resource base and the slow growth rates
imply that any increases in health expenditures derived from fiscal
financing will be slow to come without drastic changes in domestic revenue
generation capacity. This has two main consequences: first, delinking and
shifting toward a general tax–funded health system would have to be car-
ried out incrementally. Second, extension of risk pooling to the nonpoor
will have to be based on contributory risk pooling in a way that is financially self-sustainable or which at least cuts public subsidies to the nonpoor
either implicitly (for example, use of free ministry of health services) or explicitly (for example, subsidization of social security operational deficits).
This is also to ensure that LAC countries can continue urgent and priority
breadth and depth extension of risk pooling for the poor.

*Box 5.3* Mitigating the Fiscal Burden in a Transition
toward General Tax–Funded Risk Pooling:
Simulations for the Chilean Health System in 1999

Chile's experience with social insurance and a national health service dates to the early 20th century. In the early 1980s, a profound reform of social security allowed all Chileans, independent of their labor status, to choose between publicly run social health insurance (FONASA) or privately run health insurers (Instituciones de Salud Previsional [ISAPREs]). While the reform in practice allowed for risk-rated premiums for informal, self-employed, and unsalaried workers, it maintained a payroll tax contribution (7 percent of salary) for formal workers. Enrollment in a health insurance scheme is mandatory.

This dual system has created important segmentation and some equity problems. To counterbalance the incentives at the root of those problems, Chile introduced reforms beginning in 2000. Chile is also debating whether to maintain the mandatory payroll tax or transition toward a general tax–financed system. More than 35 percent of all public health expenditures are already financed from general taxation.

Baeza and Copetta (1999) explore the potential fiscal implications of shifting from a payroll tax to a risk-rated premium system with full public financing of subsidies for people who cannot afford such premiums. Instead of mandating individuals to devote a fixed amount of their salaries to buy health insurance, the authors suggest as an alternative, compulsory purchasing of a basic health insurance package with a minimum set of benefits, quality standards, and guarantees to enforce them. This benefits package (BP) would reflect societal consensus on minimum acceptable standards for a health insurance BP, quality in delivery of services, and household financial protection. The package was estimated to be equal to the current package of services offered by FONASA.

The authors demonstrate that shifting to such a system could be fiscally neutral. Payroll tax contributions are tax exempt in Chile (up to a relatively high level). Therefore, even if contributions to purchase the newly mandated BP remain tax exempt, eliminating payroll taxes increases the income tax base in a way that more than compensates for increases in fiscal expenditures to subsidize people who could not afford to pay for a risk-rated premium in either FONASA or the ISAPREs.

*Source:* Baeza and Copetta 1999.

## Shifting Toward Risk-Rated Premiums during the Transition

From the above discussion, delinking risk-pool financing from labor status (shifting away from a payroll tax) clearly could not be based on general taxation in the short run for most LAC countries. What other alternatives do policy makers have other than payroll tax–financing of risk pooling for the informal nonpoor? Not many.

Whatever mechanism is chosen has to preserve fiscal financing to extend risk pooling for the poor. This means the only option is to finance risk pooling for the nonpoor through a contributory system that also eliminates (or substantially reduces) the contribution-benefits gap—in other words, a contributory mechanism that puts the contribution close to the cost of the benefits package (or the perceived benefit) for an individual or a household. Such mechanism is known in insurance practice as a risk-rated contribution or premium.

In contrast to the payroll tax, which links contributions to a percentage of the worker's salary, risk-rated contributions link the contribution to the actuarial risk of the worker or household (as explained in chapter 3). Introducing risk-rated premiums is the most direct way of reducing the perceived gap between contribution and health benefits without public subsidization. Reference to the actuarial risk is important because it is technically impossible to achieve full risk rating. Only a fraction of the variance of individual health expenditures—up to 27 percent according to Newhouse (1998)—can be predicted in advance for individuals under full information symmetry between the insurer and the insured. In reality, premiums reflect much less individual risk than this amount and are based on the average fair actuarial cost of groups with similar actuarial characteristics such as gender, age, existing medical conditions, and recent use of health services (Baeza and Cabezas 1998). Given the asymmetry of information between the insurer and the insured, this gap will continue to exist. Therefore, in practice, risk rating aggregates individuals based on actuarial risk categories, which are averages within these groups. As a result, in addition to the economies of scale of large numbers and the implications for the variance uncertainty inherent in the calculation of the premium price, risk-rated premiums in practice allow for very significant levels of risk-pooling (as defined in chapter 1), depending on the size of the pool.

Risk rating has the advantage of narrowing the gap between contribution and perceived benefits, which could increase incentives to nonpoor informal and unsalaried workers to participate in contributory insurance. It also reduces adverse selection. From a purely risk-spreading perspective (with no equity consideration), and where risk pooling fully funded from general taxes is not feasible, risk rating is the most efficient way of financing SI for health. It allows delinking of health coverage from labor status and from the work place, and it makes it easier to get portability of benefits among risk-pooling arrangements.

Risk rating has a negative connotation among many health policy makers in LAC due to potentially significant equity problems. Indeed, reducing the contribution-benefits gap may mean that many high-risk informal and unsalaried workers would pay high premiums, so high they could not afford to pay or paying might push them into poverty. In reality, however, this group of workers does not belong to the nonpoor population as defined by figure 5.1, but to the high-risk population defined by the same figure. Today they are being subsidized either by using free MOH health services or by participating in the voluntary contributory SI schemes opened to them, or they are left to cope with their health problems, most likely falling into poverty. Therefore, this population should be treated like the high-risk population discussed above, with sufficient equity subsidies.

Shifting away from payroll taxes toward risk-rated contributions should be accompanied by active public policies to compensate for its potential equity implications. Intrinsically, risk rating, if unaccompanied by a compensatory public policy, can have significant negative equity consequences because it is not designed to address the equity objective of risk pooling.[8] Payroll taxes, in contrast, are supposed to address the risk-spreading and equity-subsidization objectives of risk pooling simultaneously (although, as discussed above, preliminary evidence suggests that SI often uses risk rating not by differentiating prices but by de facto differentiation of the benefits package) (Lenz, Volante, and Arteaga 2004).

However, in attempting to address two policy objectives (risk spreading and equity) with a single instrument, payroll taxes introduce major efficiency distortions. These include: increasing insurers' risk-selection incentives; encouraging adverse selection and incentives for nonparticipation by people who think their risk of ill health is less than the contribution would justify; and, ultimately, contributing to informality. In contrast, risk rating considers only the risk-spreading dimension. High-risk workers or households would have to pay high premiums. Lower-income households in that group might then be left out. Thus, to achieve the equity objective of risk pooling, governments shifting away from payroll tax–financed SI through risk-rated premiums should ensure explicit and well-targeted subsidization of high-risk, lower-income households, after ensuring full subsidization of the poor. Implementing a sound equity subsidy policy in this context requires mandating minimum consumption (the BP) rather than minimum spending, as is now the case in many countries under payroll tax–financed SI for health.

Most of LAC health finance systems are multiple risk-pooling systems for the nonpoor. A risk-rating premium strategy for delinking could best be achieved here, while improving equity (and efficiency and scheme financial viability) by aggregating, in advance, as many high-cost, low-probability (catastrophic) events as possible into a single risk pool, financed by all risk-pooling schemes or by fiscal proceeds only, if possible. This is known as "truncating the risk pyramid." The aggregation of catastrophic risks moves the risk burden from multiple smaller insurers to a single pool, significantly reducing both their incentives for risk selection and the cost of contributions, particularly for individuals facing these events. It can also be achieved through interpool risk-equalization funds, in which all or part of the premium is pooled and redistributed according to risk profiles of the participating risk-pooling schemes. This last solution entails significant transaction costs and technical and regulatory capacity.

In the long run, in a scenario where most of the cost of the BP would be financed by general taxation, the equity problem would be much less an issue because less and less of the BP would be financed by the risk-rated contribution.

## Improving Incentives for Participation of the Nonpoor in Contributory Risk Pooling without Delinking

In the absence of delinking, increasing the incentives for informal and un-salaried workers to participate in contributory risk-pooling schemes would require reducing the perceived contribution, increasing the perceived benefits, or both simultaneously.

The perceived cost of contributions can be reduced by realizing efficiency gains that would lower the cost of the BP, mostly through strategic purchasing and changing the incentive framework to raise the efficiency of health service providers (as discussed in chapter 4); unbundling health insurance from other SI benefits that may be less valued by individuals and households; and subsidizing the contribution cost directly or truncating the risk pyramid. Efficiency gains, truncation of the risk pyramid, and subsidization have already been discussed.

Unbundling health insurance from other less desirable benefits can reduce the contribution-benefits gap. Less desirable in practice means that the benefit is perceived as either unnecessary or unattainable. This is an important distinction, because an unnecessary benefit for a nonpoor individual may prove essential for that household, and society would end up paying the bill via public subsidies. This is often the case with high-cost, low-probability events (typically insurable events as discussed in chapter 3). Most LAC societies would not explicitly countenance denial of care to these individuals or households in case of these catastrophic health events, nor to nonpoor households that refuse to insure. That is why the minimum content of any BP commercialized in the country must be specified. A different situation arises when households perceive that the bundled benefits will never be available and that the likelihood is high they will never receive these benefits (noneffective bundled benefits).

Bundling retirement pensions with health coverage, almost universal for SI in LAC, is a prime example of ineffective bundling. Formal workers are required to contribute to retirement pensions and social health insurance simultaneously, while informal and unsalaried workers can voluntarily participate in health insurance or can get market insurance without having to contribute for an old-age pension. Retirement pensions together with social health insurance contributions in LAC cost between 15 and 30 percent of formal workers' salaries. If mandatory pension instruments are perceived to be ineffective, the contribution-benefits gap widens significantly.

Retirement pensions, notably defined-benefit systems, are often perceived as ineffective particularly by lower-income and unskilled workers who change employment status frequently and are unlikely to fulfill the minimum pension requirements if they live long enough. Other workers who prefer alternative forms of securing their welfare in old age can perceive contributions as a tax (Torche and Wagner 1997; Gill, Packard, and Yermo 2004).

The truth of the matter is that although we know that ineffective bundling can increase the contribution-benefits gap, evidence is still scarce about how much it contributes to this gap and how much it affects demand for health insurance. This is an area where experimentation, evaluation, and research are needed.[9]

But we do know that perceived benefits of participation in the social health insurance system can be increased by expanding access and improving service quality and provider responsiveness; bundling contributory risk pooling with desirable benefits (for example, disability, life, and burial insurance); improving the perceived benefits of currently bundled benefits (for example, retirement pension reform); ensuring the focus of the BP on insurable events (alignment); and increasing choice of insurance and service providers. Any one or all of these improvements could work.

# Notes

1. People living below the national poverty line in Bolivia, Chile, and Honduras (World Bank 2005).

2. In which coverage is usually linked to labor-market status and conditioned on a history of income-related contributions in the form of payroll taxes.

3. One in which the nonpoor are legally obligated to contribute earmarked funds to risk-pooling arrangements.

4. Theory suggests that at the margin, a higher contribution rate for SI distorts labor allocation if workers do not consider their contributions appropriable in the future at the market rate of interest (Corsetti 1994). When the link between mandated contributions and perceived benefits is ambiguous, SI acts simply as a tax on labor (Atkinson and Stiglitz 1980; Summers 1989).

5. Specifically, Packard (2002a) models the transition from a purely public, defined-benefit retirement security system, in which the gap between contributions and benefits is much larger, to one with private, defined-contribution individual retirement accounts that tighten the link between contributions and benefits. In addition to the negative impact on aggregate participation of high SI contributions, Packard finds a positive incentive effect after the introduction of individual retirement accounts that, holding other determining factors constant, increases the share of the economically active population who contribute to the reformed pension system.

6. For example, tutelas in Colombia, where individuals use legal mechanisms originally designed to protect citizens' rights (tutela) to obtain free health care services from the government to which they are not entitled.

7. Although in some Latin American countries, such as Argentina and Brazil, unsalaried workers are also mandated to contribute through payroll taxes.

8. For an extensive review of this problem see Baeza and Cabezas (1999).

9. Other similar examples of ineffective bundling include benefits on housing loans, access to recreational facilities, and short-term consumer loans.

# 6

# The Quest for Efficiency and Universal Coverage: Health Sector Reform in Latin America and the Caribbean

THE LAST TWO DECADES have seen an abundance of health system reforms in Latin America and the Caribbean (LAC). Most countries have attempted major reforms mainly in revenue collection, risk pooling (including health insurance), and purchasing, but some countries have also made attempts in health service delivery. Several governments have succeeded in implementing these reforms, while many have not yet met their objectives.

In this chapter, we examine key health sector reforms in the LAC region during the last two decades. Our discussion is organized around two main objectives, proposed here as the central pillars of health reform in the region: the quest to extend effective health care coverage to all (universal coverage), and the search to improve health system efficiency in financing and delivering services. Although we discuss these objectives separately for analytical purposes, the motivation for many of these reforms is deeply rooted in both. Thus, the separation of the two may strike some readers as somewhat contrived.

Despite growing interest and debate in the region, reforms to delink health system financing from labor market status and to unbundle health insurance from pension mandates (discussed in chapter 5) are notoriously absent from the reform agenda. No country in the region has yet launched a delinking or an unbundling reform. Implementing either of the two, particularly delinking, would entail overcoming the formidable challenges discussed in chapter 5 and at the end of this chapter.

This chapter is organized in two sections. Universal coverage and efficiency-enhancing reforms are reviewed in the first section. The second section summarizes the emerging lessons from both types of reforms, including the lack of evidence regarding what works and what does not; the complex political economy of regulating private insurers and reforming public service providers, particularly to introduce flexibility in health service personnel management; and the financial sustainability of reforms, particularly the fiscal challenges, and the complex political economy of related tax reform.

Achieving universal coverage has been a long-standing objective of most LAC countries. The core objective of achieving universal coverage has been to ensure access to health services for all (increasingly represented as guaranteeing a package of basic services or benefits). None of these reforms—with the possible exceptions of Mexico in 2003 and Chile in 2004—has been explicitly directed at ensuring financial protection.

Public policy toward universal coverage in Latin America can be traced back to the 1910s and 1920s when Bismarck-type social insurance (SI) systems were introduced in the region to cover formal workers. Then, as complements to social insurance, national health services (NHSs), delivered directly through ministries of health, were created in the 1940s, 1950s, and 1960s to provide the poor and uninsured with health service coverage. Before that, providing basic health coverage to workers and the poor was essentially a private endeavor supported through the multiple beneficence organizations active in the region until the early 20th century.

Some key examples of universal coverage reforms include the NHS reforms (Chile 1952); the creation of the Sistema Unico de Saude (Unified Health System) in Brazil in the late 1980s; the integration of social security and the Ministry of Health in Costa Rica in the mid 1990s; and the Colombian health insurance reform of 1994. More recent reforms include the maternal and child insurance reforms in Bolivia (1998), Peru (1999), and Argentina (2003); the Seguro Popular de Salud reform in Mexico (2003); and the Universal Guaranteed Coverage (AUGE) reform in Chile in 2004.

The main challenges raised in the debate on achieving universal coverage in the region revolve around the operational meaning of universal coverage and the type of risk-pooling arrangement through which it is best achieved.[1] The first challenge centers on the depth versus breadth tradeoff for extending coverage. The second challenge refers to the question of whether shifting from one risk-pooling arrangement to another counts as extension of coverage. Implicitly, this discussion is just another phase in the long-standing debate regarding the Bismarck versus Beveridge approaches to structuring SI, a debate that is very much alive in the LAC region. In addition, particularly in middle-income countries, there is a trend toward introducing explicit entitlements (benefits packages [BPs]) in conjunction with the push for universal coverage.

Improving the efficiency of health systems is not only the objective (often not explicit) of many reforms in LAC countries, but also essential to achieving universal coverage where resources are scarce. Like the debate over universal coverage, discussions about improving efficiency have also been going on for some time in LAC countries. In fact, the creation of most national health services, as was the case with the British National Health Service in the mid 1940s, responded to a consensus that a unified and coordinated health system would meet country needs more efficiently than the fragmented beneficence systems that were prevalent in most countries in the early 20th century.

In the United Kingdom, World War II was a catalyst to building consensus for the creation of the NHS. In LAC countries, other events were the catalyst. For example, the 1938 earthquake in Chile catalyzed policy discussion, culminating in the foundation of the NHS in 1952. Later on, in the 1960s, 1970s, and early 1980s, the search for efficiency was closely focused on implementing and scaling up cost-effective programs and a more cost-effective health service delivery model in LAC. Considerable effort in public health policy since then has been devoted to increasing basic cost-effectiveness of public health programs (for example, extending coverage of vaccine programs, which made Latin America the first developing region to eradicate polio) and to establishing increasingly complex networks of providers as a way of resolving patients' health concerns as early as possible and at the lowest cost. The best example of such efforts has been the primary health care strategy implemented in the LAC region.

Since the early 1990s, reforms to improve health system efficiency in the region have focused most notoriously on health financing. Health financing reform faces two main challenges: reducing systemic fragmentation, especially in risk pooling, and creating the right incentive framework for efficient health service delivery and equitable and efficient risk pooling.

To reduce fragmentation, LAC country policy debate has centered around two key policy options: to seek reform that merges all risk-pooling organizations into one (for example, Costa Rica's reform in the mid 1990s), or to aim for a virtual single pool, allowing multiple risk-pooling organizations to coexist, but under a common regulatory framework (for example, Colombia 1994, Brazil late 1980s, and Chile 2004).

Reforms to create the right incentive framework for insurers and health service providers include strengthening the purchaser-provider compact by splitting purchaser-provider functions and initiating provider-payment reforms; introducing public-private competition for the delivery of mandatory health insurance and publicly financed health services; and reorganizing public and social security service providers.

Although few, if any, of the reforms attempt explicitly to improve the alignment of priorities and instruments (discussed in chapter 3), the thrust to spread risk pooling (achieve universal coverage) does aim at such an alignment. LAC households spend too much out-of-pocket on health, both in absolute terms and as compared to other predominately middle-income country regions (discussed in chapter 2). A better balance has to be achieved between health finance through individual saving, which is too high in the region, and risk pooling, which is too low.

## Achieving Universal Coverage

The universal coverage agenda now predominates health reform debate in most LAC countries, but its meaning is still evolving. What is universal coverage? The current debate follows three main avenues involving the tradeoff between breadth and depth of coverage; the type of risk-pooling arrangement for achieving universal coverage (that is, the Bismarck versus Beveridge type); and the challenge of extending coverage to the informal sector (explored at length in chapter 5).

### Coverage as Breadth and Depth

In a variation from Kutzin's (2001) proposed definition of breadth and depth, we use breadth of coverage in reference to the number of people who have access to basic health services. Depth refers to the quality of the health BP, the interventions included in the package, and the technical characteristics involved in the delivery of those services. Under budget constraints, the necessary tradeoffs between the two can be overcome only by efficiency gains. This inevitable link between universal coverage and efficiency-enhancing reforms is discussed next.

Most LAC countries have had to confront the depth versus breadth tradeoff at some point in building their health systems. Other regions have also faced the same policy tradeoff (box 6.1). The SI schemes created for formal workers in LAC in the early 20th century were based on the depth of coverage option—many services for a small proportion of the population (there were fewer formal workers than today). National health service arrangements embody the choice for breadth in their attempt to reach the entire population but, bowing to financial constraints, with a much shallower BP than is typically offered by SI plans. In this context, extending coverage or achieving universal coverage has a different meaning in low- and lower middle-income countries than in higher middle-income countries.

*Box 6.1* South Korea and Taiwan: From Fragmentation to Universal Coverage through Social Insurance— Reforms and Breadth versus Depth Choices

South Korea and Taiwan are paradigmatic cases of SI reforms that have led to universal risk pooling.

The expansion of health insurance in the Republic of Korea began with the government developing a planning process that first considered expanding the benefits of the shallow package that was available to the population covered. Subsequently the government focused on a longer term process for progressive expansion of coverage to all workers and their families in both the formal and informal sectors. Undoubtedly, a prolonged period of persistent economic growth created the appropriate fiscal environment. By the mid 1970s, roughly 9 percent of the population was covered by formal social insurance (Peabody, Lee, and Bickel 1995). In 1977, two programs were established: the Free and Subsidized Medical Aid Program with a small package of benefits for low income families, and a health insurance program for workers and their families employed by firms with more than 500 employees. Expansion was gradually introduced to firms with a smaller number of employees, and later public employees. During the mid 1980s, more than 40 percent of the population was covered and by 1987 almost 80 percent of the population was covered. By the mid 1990s, virtually all of the population had health insurance coverage.

The process of expanding health insurance coverage began in Taiwan with the analysis of the experience of a successful pilot program for farmers implemented at the end of the 1980s. In the early 1990s, the government developed a national agenda for expanding health insurance to the rest of the population. This agenda was developed with the results of a series of studies that proposed a plan to expand the population covered and the package of benefits gradually over a period of more than 10 years. By 1995, the government introduced a major piece of legislation to expand health insurance. In the year before the legislation was passed, 57 percent of the population of Taiwan was covered by one of the three major public health insurance programs, and only one year later more than 90 percent of the population was covered. Although the expansion may seem unexpectedly explosive (breadth), several authors have pointed out the importance of the lessons learned from pilot projects, the extremely meticulous analysis of financial and economic feasibility, as well as the budgetary implications. Political events catalyzed the implementation of a process that was well under way. In addition, the economic growth achieved in the decade previous to the expansion of health insurance provided important fiscal space for authorities to respond to the pressing demand of wide sectors of the population.

*Source:* Baeza, Montenegro, and Núñez 2002.

In lower-income countries (for example, Bolivia, Haiti, Honduras, Nicaragua, and Paraguay), where formal employment occupies a small part of the labor force and fiscal constraints are substantial, universal coverage is focused on breadth rather than depth. The scarcity of resources makes it essential for policy makers to match health sector priorities (interventions that need to reach the whole population with the limited resources available) to the best available policy instruments to protect households (discussed in chapter 3). In other words, it is essential to ensure the right combination of prevention, saving, and risk-pooling instruments, reserving the latter for insurable events. Because scarcity demands efficiency gains, most reform efforts have concentrated on ensuring that at least a basic package of services reaches everyone, particularly the poor. Examples of this strategy include maternal and child insurance programs (in effect, fully subsidized noncontributory benefits packages) introduced in Bolivia and Peru in the late 1990s and recently in Ecuador, Nicaragua, Paraguay, and elsewhere.

In upper middle-income countries (for example, Argentina, Brazil, Chile, Colombia, Mexico, and Uruguay), achieving universal coverage is more closely related to depth of coverage than to breadth, even though there are continuing efforts to extend protection to the remaining population pockets with still very limited access. The number of services, as well as their quality, is at the center of the coverage agenda. In addition, momentum is building for introducing the BP as an explicit entitlement. This is part of an effort to link health care to the rights guaranteed to all citizens. It also seems part of an attempt to provide every member of society, particularly the poor, with the instruments to secure state compliance with these specific entitlements. This approach, in its specificity, contrasts with the nebulous, traditional, universal right to health set forth in the constitutions of most LAC countries, but without giving citizens any instrument for forcing the state to deliver on this promise. In light of this trend, what are the implications for future reforms in the LAC region?

In both low- and middle-income countries, the challenge of reaching and including the nonpoor informal sector in the extension of contributory risk pooling is essential. In low-income countries it is particularly important to ensure that the very scarce resources are effectively targeted to increase risk pooling for the poor. In middle-income countries, it is important because it is often the last segment missing to achieve universal coverage.

## Reshaping Health Benefits Packages as Explicit Entitlements

The constitutions of most LAC countries mandate citizens' rights to good health or access to health services, but not until the mid 1990s were these mandates translated into effective instruments for the poor to demand compliance by the state or other health system actors. First Colombia in 1994, and since then, Argentina (1996, Obras Sociales), Chile (2003), Mexico (2003), Argentina (2003, public sector), and Ecuador (2004) have introduced legislation and sector reforms to transform health BP into explicit entitlements guaranteed to all citizens. Such reforms also include legal mechanisms for beneficiaries to demand state compliance. The introduction of such explicit entitlements is having multiple intended and unexpected effects.

First, it has forced a revisit of the breadth and depth discussion that many middle-income countries thought they had solved. Before the reforms, all services were theoretically available to every citizen (a deep BP). In practice, however, nothing was guaranteed (often resulting in a shallow package, particularly for the poor). Now, under the explicit entitlement reforms, as BPs become legally binding on governments, the debate over whether to guarantee a limited package or a deep package (often focused on protecting households from impoverishing health shocks) is very much alive. Second, the entitlement reforms have forced a much closer dialogue between ministries of finance and ministries of health because the legally binding nature of the packages shrinks the space for fiscal adjustment at the expense of the health sector, depending on the breadth and depth of the package and on the indexation mechanism between fiscal transfers and package costs. Errors in defining the package can have far-reaching consequences on the financial, particularly fiscal, sustainability of the reform. Third, though unintended, most reforms have provided governments with a powerful instrument for achieving efficiency-enhancing reforms without losing public support. Guaranteeing a package requires clarity and certainty regarding the quality of services delivered, which in turn requires complex monitoring systems and provider-payment systems with contracts or quasi-contracts between the public financing agency and health service providers. All these features hinge on effective purchasing.

The most interesting feature of explicit entitlement reforms is that they seem to require implementation of most of the efficiency-enhancing reforms, but they include them as instruments subordinated to the goal of guaranteeing the package rather than as objectives of the reform in themselves. This is a significant departure from the almost purely efficiency-enhancing reforms of the 1990s, focused mainly on the instruments (for example, payment mechanisms or granting autonomy to providers or the purchasing agency) rather than on the specific benefits for the target population. Consensus is growing in the LAC health system debate that stressing reform instruments rather than benefits in the 1990s might have undermined public support for reforms.

Examples of explicit entitlement reforms include the Colombian Plan Obligatorio de Salud (POS, mandatory BP) introduced in 1994; the 1996 Argentine Plan Medico Obligatorio (PMO, mandatory BP) and the 2003 Plan Nacer (Universal Maternal and Child BP); the Chilean Plan de Acceso Universal con Garantias Explicitas (AUGE, mandated, universal, state-guaranteed BP) introduced in 2003; and the Mexican CASES (Catálogo de Servicios Esenciales de Salud) introduced in 2003.

Colombia introduced a substantial reform of its social health insurance system in 1994. Under the new system, the state mandates a benefits package for all payroll tax payers and guarantees, through demand-side public subsidies for insurance (including also financing of one-percentage point of contributors from the Régimen Contributivo participants), a BP (POS) for the poor (Régimen Subsidiado). Colombia was the first country in the region to introduce a guaranteed explicit BP for the poor. The literature on the Colombian reform underlines the enormous technical and regulatory challenge of enforcing the guaranteed BP for the poor in a reform of such complexity.

Argentina's PMO was introduced as an explicit entitlement for beneficiaries of its SI system (Obras Sociales Nacionales, OSN). The PMO covers the mostly nonpoor formal sector, but the few evaluations of the impact of PMO on the lowest income OSN beneficiaries show that the mere existence of the PMO, in the absence of effective regulation and enforcement, does not guarantee that lower-income OSN members actually fully benefit from the package. The case of the Argentine PMO also confirms the enormous technical, political, and regulatory challenge of the explicit entitlement approach. In part as a result of these lessons, since 2003 Argentina has been introducing a guaranteed BP for a segment of the poor population (uninsured mothers and children), a package of basic maternal and child services (Conjunto de Prestaciones Basicas, CPB). This reform is still in its preliminary stage of design and implementation.

Chile's explicit health insurance BP, AUGE, was tested first in a small pilot project among the population covered by the national health service (Fondo Nacional de Salud [FONASA]) in 2002 and 2003. The pilot showed improved access of the target population to the services included in the package. Since July 1, 2005, AUGE has been mandatory for all citizens and all public and private insurers. The Chilean reform is still too preliminary for evaluation, and there is little evidence on its impact in general or on the poor. The AUGE package sets maximum waiting times and minimum quality standards for the services included in the package. It also sets a vast array of monitoring systems and complaint mechanisms. However, a preliminary assessment showed, as in the case of Colombia and Argentina, the enormous technical and regulatory challenges that Chile faces for the AUGE implementation.

Mexico has been implementing the Seguro Popular de Salud (SPS) in the states since 2001. This is a voluntary public insurance scheme for the people not covered by social security. Its target population is around half the Mexican population, giving coverage priority to families in the poorest income quintile. In 2001–3, the SPS was run as a program led by the Ministry of Health. It started in five pilot states, and by the end of 2003, 22 states had joined the program. As of January 2004, the SPS has been implemented under the aegis and rules of the General Health Law after Congress approved a reform in 2003 that established it formally as a public health insurance mechanism. The SPS affiliation process is gradual over a seven-year span. Universal coverage of its target population is intended for 2010. The SPS began operations as a pilot program at the end of 2001. Since it began operating as a formal health insurance in 2004 through the first half of 2005, it has covered 2,071,512 families (6,871,263 individuals), representing 11.9 percent of the total target population.

The SPS has a tripartite financial scheme comprising contributions paid on a per family basis by the federal and state governments—both from general taxation as well as income-tested family contributions. Families in the lowest income quintile do not contribute but are responsible for participating actively in preventive health care. The allocation of resources is based on the principle of subsidizing demand rather than supply. The SPS is supervised by the Federal Ministry of Health (Secretaría de Salud) and managed by the states. Services are provided by a network of accredited public providers in each state. SPS includes an explicit guaranteed BP (CASES) of essential services and drugs focused mainly on primary health care and general hospitalization. The CASES covers 85 percent of the most frequently demanded services such as antenatal care (child delivery), as well as detection and ambulatory care for diabetes. There is also a package of services considered as catastrophic for the operation of the SPS (Catálogo del Fondo de Protección contra Gastos Catastróficos, CFPGC). These services are funded through a national pool of 8 percent of all federal and state contributions to the SPS. Third parties can also contribute to this fund.[2]

## Bismarck versus Beveridge: Does It Matter?

Some specialists and policy makers are tempted to assume that people are not covered by a risk-pooling mechanism just because they receive their health care through the NHS and do not participate in formal contributory health insurance (social or private). In fact, participants in the LAC policy debate often succumb to this temptation. The implication is that coverage under NHS arrangements means not being covered at all by risk-pooling arrangements.

As discussed in chapters 1 and 4, the risk-pooling function can be organized in different ways. These alternatives include both the Bismarck-type contributory social health insurance and the Beveridge-type NHS arrangement. In the former, risk pooling is done within the pool of contributors via payroll tax. In the latter, risk pooling occurs at the societal level, and all tax-paying citizens contribute through general taxation. Countries have opted for one or the other more by historical accident than by explicit choice. In Europe, the decision was based on historical, cultural, and political conditions when the health systems were founded at the end of the 19th century and early in the 20th century. Countries like Germany, the Netherlands, Austria, and others followed the Bismarck SI model of 1882. Others such as Sweden, the United Kingdom, and Norway followed the Beveridge NHS model of the 1940s. Countries in LAC have always been greatly influenced by European health system trends. As a result, most countries in the region have both social security for formal workers and the NHS for the rest of the population. Therefore, except for the low-income LAC countries, most others have a fairly good breadth, but unequal depth of coverage among different segments of the population.

What then do covered and uncovered mean when talking about populations in LAC? The covered versus uncovered debate, besides the payroll tax policy debate extensively reviewed in chapter 5, seems to relate more to value judgments regarding the efficiency and quality of the NHS as compared to SI arrangements. It also includes a separate, but often ill-supported vision that moving from NHS to SI-type arrangements would reduce differences in depth of coverage between participants in the respective systems.

Would LAC countries achieve universal coverage if they could suddenly move the entire population from the NHS to a SI scheme? If they could, the income constraints of households under NHS would most likely prevent them from being able to contribute and would require large public subsidies (as does the NHS). Most likely, too, given fiscal constraints, the overall amount of public subsidy would be unchanged. Thus, the BP would remain similar to the current one under the NHS, except for efficiency gains or for full pooling of funds among formal workers, newly included poor, and informal workers within social security (equivalent to societal pooling).

So what difference does it make? Beyond the large per capita expenditures either way and the payroll tax distortionary effects, it is not clear that only risk-pooling arrangement characteristics determine differences between the two systems. The differences in the depth of coverage between the poor and the nonpoor have much to do with fiscal constraints, efficiency of the purchasing function, and the political economy of tax reforms and much less to do with the type of risk-pooling arrangement chosen.

In addition, what seems to be the basis for the implicit judgment about NHS—(in)efficiency—is related mostly to the occasional existence of a strategic purchasing function, explicit contracting, and explicit provider-payment mechanisms under SI organizations. Strategic purchasing arrangements are the exception rather than the rule for both SI and NHS organizations in the LAC region. It is true, however, that SI organizations tend to include more often explicit contracting and production-based payment systems, thus possibly the source of confusion. However, when these preliminary forms of strategic purchasing exist either in SI or NHS, they are too often defeated by the complexity of governance arrangements and the political economy of these quasi-public organizations and their relations with their service providers. These complexities are similar under both systems, and in reality little is known in LAC about their comparative efficiency or productivity. In LAC, both SI and NHS arrangements need to introduce significant strategic purchasing reforms (for example, provider-payment reforms, separation of provision and purchasing) that go hand-in-hand with governance arrangements that will allow for the full realization of their potential. Some of the latest reforms in the region are introducing these purchasing reforms. Then, at this stage in the health reform process in the region, more important than the Bismarck- or Beveridge-model debate, is that these strategic purchasing and governance reforms should be fully implemented in both types of arrangements.

What really matters in achieving universal coverage is ensuring that the whole population has access to acceptable health services (as defined by society) and financial protection. The type of risk-pooling arrangements put in place to do so is instrumental and will most likely evolve at different moments in a country's economic and social life. In this context, policy makers would be well advised to avoid spending so much government political capital on moving households from one arrangement to another without looking closely at what these transfers will do to expand service access and financial protection, particularly for the poor and people at risk of health care poverty. In assessing alternatives they might well conclude that the strategic purchasing and governance reforms have potentially a more promising impact as first steps in improving access to services and financial protection at this stage of the system development.

## Improving Health Sector Efficiency in Latin America and the Caribbean

Though less explicitly, the pursuit of increased health system efficiency complemented the universal coverage agenda in the region during the 1990s. Since the late 1980s and early 1990s, reforms to improve health system efficiency in the LAC region have focused most notoriously on health financing reforms. There are two main challenges for health financing reform: reducing systemic fragmentation, particularly in risk pooling, and creating the right incentive framework for efficient health service delivery.

## Reducing Fragmentation: Single versus Virtual Single Risk-Pool

Health systems in LAC countries are fragmented and segmented. Fragmentation and segmentation severely hamper health system performance on efficiency and equity. *Fragmentation* is defined as a multiplicity of often small and incentive-conflicting risk-pooling organizations, with little or no portability of benefits among them and unequal and discretionary access to direct and indirect public subsidies. In addition, the limited extent of risk pooling (high out-of-pocket expenditures) also contributes to fragmentation because high out-of-pocket spending means risk pooling at the lowest possible level, the household. *Segmentation* refers to the separation of subgroups of the covered population as a result of incentives or regulatory frameworks under different risk-pooling arrangements. Typical examples of such segmentation are differential risk-pooling arrangements by labor status (formal workers covered by SI, informal poor covered by the NHS, and informal better-off covered by voluntary private health insurance).

Fragmentation reduces efficiency because large risk pools entail reductions in their costs of financial reserves as a proportion of total revenue (mostly due to a reduction in the variance of expected health expenditures). This means lower financial costs and more resources available to pay for health services. Usually large pools are also better able than small pools to implement successful purchasing strategies vis-à-vis health service providers. In addition, fragmentation severely hampers households' ability to protect themselves: first, due to limited risk pooling (and consequently high out-of-pocket spending), and second, because the lack of portable benefits often leaves people without coverage when moving from one locality to another, changing jobs, or moving in and out of the formal labor market as often the most vulnerable households do.

Segmentation also reduces systemic efficiency and equity, particularly when a large part of segmentation results from linking labor status with financing and participation in a particular risk-pooling scheme (for example, social security or the NHS). In this case, a job change often means a change in benefits eligibility and large gaps in continuity. It might even introduce rigidities into the labor market, as happens with employer-based health insurance (which is still rare in Latin America).

For households, segmentation is also a problem. It often means that changes in labor status would result not only in an increased contribution to the health system (informal workers usually do not pay payroll taxes), but also in lost public subsidies (usually given to poor households in-kind only through the NHS). This is not just an equity problem for low-income workers; it might also deter them from seeking formal employment.

Efficiency-enhancing reforms therefore need to reduce fragmentation and segmentation in the health system. The challenges to do so are enormous. These range from the political economy issues related to merging organizations and changing long-standing regulations on benefits and the portability of public subsidies beyond public providers, to the fiscal and technical complexities of restructuring public and social security providers, and to the political economy of such restructuring. (We discuss most of these in the last section of this chapter.) Thus, although most policy makers in the LAC region know that fragmentation and segmentation must be reduced, few reforms have moved forward in this regard. Exceptions include Costa Rica with the merging of the Ministry of Health and social security in the mid 1990s, Brazil with the creation of the Unified Health System in the late 1980s and early 1990s, Colombia with Law 100 in 1994, and Chile with the merging of social security and the NHS (creating FONASA) in the mid 1980s.

In reducing fragmentation and segmentation, LAC countries face a strategic decision regarding single or multiple risk pools. Should they try to reduce fragmentation by consolidating all risk pools in a single risk-pooling organization, or should they maintain multiple risk-pooling organizations but aggregate them in a virtual single pool?[3] Policy debate has been intense regarding these two options, reflecting each country's historic and cultural background as well as tensions and visions that go beyond technical and efficiency issues.

No doubt this debate has been very important in the reform discussions in countries as different as Uruguay and Mexico. Should Mexico opt in the long run for concentrating the risk-pooling function in only one national organization (for example, Instituto Mexicano de Seguridad Social [IMSS]) and restructure all of the state health systems as service providers in competition with other public and private providers? Or, should Mexico choose instead to have multiple risk-pooling organizations (for example, IMSS, Instituto de Seguridad y Servicios Sociales para los Trabajadores del Estado [ISSSTE], Seguro Popular, private insurers)? The answer for Mexico, with 120 million inhabitants, might be totally different from the solution for Uruguay, with 3 million inhabitants. Should Uruguay keep its multiplicity of risk-pooling organizations (for example, Mutual Health Insurance Organizations [IAMCs], State Health Service Administration [ASSE], and Direccion de Seguros

Sociales por Enfermedad [DISSE]) or, considering the small size of its risk pool, should it merge all the organizations into a single pool? These are not rhetorical questions; they are at the core of policy options in many LAC countries.

Opinions (as there is still a significant lack of evidence in this debate) are greatly divided in LAC. Some favor the merged single-pool option; others prefer the virtual single-pool option. For proponents of an actual single-pool organization, creating a single, large risk pool would ensure both risk and equity subsidization much more efficiently. Large pools, in some cases national pools, greatly facilitate effective and efficient cross-subsidization among groups with different incomes and health risks. In that context, multiple pooling organizations, particularly if they compete with each other, entail the risk of further risk-pool fragmentation, increased inefficiencies and inequities due to market failure, and lack of risk and equity cross-subsidization. Proponents also argue that regulation and incentives to counterbalance such problems are institutionally and technically complex and entail high transaction costs. Costa Rica is the best example of a LAC country that chose the single-pool option (and merged its national health and SI systems into a single pool in the mid 1990s).

For supporters of the virtual single-pool option (through any combination of organizational arrangement but often including private health insurance), this strategy simply reflects reality in most LAC countries where multiple arrangements coexist and, financially and politically, would be extremely costly to merge. They also argue that public monopolies in health pose significant efficiency problems and are often subject to policy function capture by sector unions or others. For supporters, this makes it essential to bring into the discussion of actual versus virtual single pools, not only the potential inefficiencies of a multiple-pool competing system, but also the inefficiencies derived from governance and microefficiency limitations of public monopolies. Examples of countries that have chosen the virtual single-pool option include Colombia (which introduced a comprehensive multiple-pool reform in 1993) (Londoño 1996), Brazil (late 1980s), and Chile (which began a third generation of reforms for virtual pool integration in 2004) (Baeza 1998).

Evidence is lacking regarding which of the two best achieves effective financial protection through universal risk pooling and has the most impact on access to services. Therefore, we do not endorse any of these strategies in particular as the solution or sole strategy for achieving universal coverage. Policy makers instead should strive to improve health and financial protection for all, particularly for the poor, using any and all strategies or instruments proven to work in their country context.

## Creating the Right Incentive Framework for Insurers and Service Providers

Reforms to create the right incentive framework for insurers and health service providers include strengthening the purchaser-provider compact by splitting up the purchaser and provider functions and by reforming provider-payment systems; introducing public-private competition for the delivery of mandatory health insurance and the delivery of publicly financed health services; and reconverting (reorganizing) NHS and social security service providers.

Although few, if any, of the reforms explicitly attempt to improve matching of priorities and instruments (discussed in chapter 3), the strong push to increase risk pooling does. LAC households spend too much out-of-pocket on health in absolute terms and as compared to other predominately middle-income country regions (discussed in chapter 2). Countries also need to achieve a better balance between self-insurance, too high in the LAC region, and risk pooling, too low by any measure. Table 6.1 summarizes some of the main efficiency-enhancing reforms in the region since 1980.

Reforms to create the right incentive framework for insurers and service providers in LAC—so crucial for the future performance of health systems—are still evolving and have proven technically and politically complex. At the core of such complexity is the problem of historical capture of public subsidies (in the case of NHS) or most financial proceeds (in the case of social security) by their own network of providers within an integrated network. Introducing accountability mechanisms for provider productivity and ultimately linking payment to service delivery can have significant negative consequences for nonperforming providers, which makes the reforms less palatable to powerful health sector unions. This explains a good part of the political complexity of these reforms. We further discuss this complexity in the second section of this chapter.

## Strengthening the Purchaser-Provider Compact

Most countries in the region have attempted to strengthen the purchaser-provider compact through the introduction of purchaser-provider split and contractual and payment mechanisms to create the right incentive framework for providers.

Purchasing and provision are usually integrated in most NHS and social security organizations in Latin America. Under such integration, the central authority has the simultaneous mission of maximizing the impact of their resources on the participant population, of financing the system, and of ensuring financial viability of their own providers. Historically,

*Table 6.1* Country Cases: Efficiency-Enhancing Reforms in Latin America and the Caribbean, 1980–2004

| Type of Reform | Specific Reform | Country | Feature |
|---|---|---|---|
| Strengthening the purchaser-provider compact in the national health service and social security | Purchaser-provider split | • Uruguay (1998)<br>• Argentina (1997)<br>• Chile (1981, 1997)<br>• Colombia (1994)<br>• Mexico (2003) | • Strengthening of State Health Service Administration, (ASSE) as the purchasing agency, Uruguay<br>• Salta and Mendoza health sector reforms in the late 1990s<br>• Creation of FONASA in the early 1980s and its consolidation as the public sector purchasing agency in the late 1990s, Chile<br>• Creation of Seguro Popular de Salud as the purchasing agency |
| | Public provider-payment reforms | • Costa Rica (1995)<br>• Chile (1985, 1992)<br>• Brazil (1985)<br>• Nicaragua (1998) | • Payment reforms within the Caja Costarricense de Seguro Social<br>• Municipal primary health care capitation and FONASA-NHS payment reforms<br>• Contracting and payment reforms for contracting out with private providers<br>• Budget decentralization and performance agreements |

142

| | | | |
|---|---|---|---|
| Introducing public-private competition | Private-public competition for mandated health insurance | • Chile (1985)<br>• Colombia (1994) | • Instituciones de Salud Previsional (ISAPREs)<br>• Empresas Promotoras de Salud (EPSs) |
| | Demand-side subsidy for insurance | • Colombia (1994) | • Subsidized modality in the social health insurance reform |
| | Private-public competition for the provision of publicly financed health services | • Chile (1985)<br>• Argentina (Salta 2001) | • FONASA voucher system<br>• Outsourcing public hospital management to the private sector (Hospital Materno-Infantil) |
| Reconverting public providers | Direct community participation in governance of public providers | • Panama (1999)<br>• Perú (1990s)<br>• Bolivia (1990s) | • San Miguelito Hospital<br>• CLAS<br>• Decentralization to municipal level for the maternal and child insurance |
| | Public hospital autonomy | • Argentina (1994)<br>• Colombia (1994)<br>• Uruguay (1998)<br>• Panama (1999)<br>• Chile (2003) | |

Abbreviations: See pp. xxi–xx.
*Source:* Author.

*Box 6.2* United Kingdom: Strengthening the Purchaser-
          Provider Compact through Internal Market Reforms

The National Health Service (NHS) reform in the United Kingdom is probably the paradigm of strengthening the purchaser-provider compact through internal market reforms in the public sector. The reform was laid out initially in the White Paper of the Conservative Government in 1989 (Department of Health 1989). Basically, the reform sought to separate purchasing from provision. The purchasing function was given to the NHS, which decentralized the function to regional Health Authorities (HAs). In addition, the role of physician general practitioners (GPs) changed, and they increasingly acted simultaneously as providers of primary care and family medicine for patients joining their practice and as purchasers of some more complex services from public hospitals for their patients. This structure was called GP Fund Holders (GPFH). The proportion of GPFHs increased during the 1990s. Provision then was done by GPs and also by public hospitals that would be transformed into autonomous hospitals (NHS Trusts). NHS Trusts were given quite a bit of flexibility to allow them, for example, to seek private financing for investments. However, in practice, personnel management was always restricted throughout the reform.

Some analysts believe that internal market reforms were never fully implemented in the United Kingdom due to many central government restrictions in the model for both purchasers and providers. Similarly, Maynard (1994) argued that there was an internal contradiction in the reform policy illustrated by the lack of a clear development strategy for the GPFHs, which were key elements in the new structure; weak definitions of the price and contract rules; and absence of personnel management authority for the NHS Trusts. He also suggested that although the reform had potential and made more explicit to all actors in the system that improvements in the allocation of resources were needed, the results of the competition, as implemented in the UK reforms of the 1990s, were much less clear than optimists had predicted at the outset. Transaction costs within the system actually increased administrative costs.

Views regarding the performance and impact of the reforms vary (Maynard 1994; OECD 1992; Robinson and Le Grand 1994; and World Bank 1997). Robinson and Le Grand argue that the impact on efficiency has been positive and that there probably were gains through the introduction of GPFH. However, in the case of the NHS Trusts, the efficiency gains were related to changes in process and not to the specific changes in the trust system. Evidence suggests that the problems connected with the 1990s reforms were concentrated in four areas: high political and administrative costs of introducing the reform; some increasing inequities, particularly between patients in the GPFH scheme and nonmembers; and

*(Box continues on the following page.)*

*Box 6.2* (continued)

increasingly perverse incentives for NHS Trusts to increase production of services.

Since 1998 with the election of a new Labour government, important reforms have been introduced. The new government downplayed the importance of competition in the NHS and significantly changed the purchasing function, including the elimination of GPFH and its replacement by GP groups (Primary Care Groups, PCGs) to replace the GPFH, in theory eliminating some of the perverse incentives in the GPFH. Some GPFHs became too small a risk pool and also received risk-selection incentives. The main changes in 1998 included the introduction of guidelines and standards for health services based on data and cost-effectiveness; new emphasis on quality through the PCGs and improvement of quality standards for longer term contracts; and the implementation of a regulation commission within the NHS (the Commission for Health Improvements) to act as regulator and moderator in internal market problems.

*Source:* Adapted from Baeza and Cabezas 1998.

that combination of missions has created incentives for the central authority (either the NHS or social security) to focus on ensuring a stable flow of revenue to their own providers rather than on the impact on the population. Both NHS and SI usually have large networks of their own providers: hospitals and outpatient centers. Thus, the separation of purchaser and provider attempts to create within the system an agent capable of concentrating on maximizing value for money, no matter who provides a service. Without such an agent, the organization tends to focus more on financing its own providers than on getting value for money. It is difficult for an integrated agent to put pressure on its own providers, because any financial difficulty of theirs would ultimately become its own responsibility. A potential problem with the purchaser-provider split is some loss of cost control if control over budget execution is not tight enough.

Strengthening the purchaser-provider compact also entails implementing provider-payment mechanisms, including contracting within the public sector, contracting out with the private sector, and introducing performance agreements. These mechanisms attempt a shift from historically supply-side provider financing toward production-based provider payments. In other words, they aim at linking payment of providers with services currently delivered to the population instead of basing current payments on past costs.

Most health reforms in Latin America since 1990 have included some or all elements of strengthening the purchaser-provider compact. The most notable reforms include: the Brazilian reform of provider-payment mechanisms in the late 1980s; the second generation of reforms in FONASA in Chile in the 1990s; the Colombia insurance reform in the mid 1990s; and in the late 1990s, the Costa Rica Social Security reform, the Peruvian Integrated Health Insurance Reform (SIS), the Nicaraguan Local Integrated Health Care System (SILAIS) strengthening, the ASSE reforms of the current introduction of Maternal and Child Insurance in Argentina, and the Seguro Popular in Mexico.

## Reconverting Public and Social Security Providers

To reorganize public and social security providers in the region, two nonmutually exclusive approaches have been taken: the introduction of public hospital autonomy and direct community participation in provider management and governance.

Attempts to introduce hospital autonomy were most prevalent in the reform of health service provisions in the LAC region during the 1990s. *Autonomy* refers to the authority given to public providers (or social security providers) for self-governance, including the management of most production factors. This reform follows the concept of hospital trusts set forth by the NHS reforms in the United Kingdom in the early 1990s. Although there is no single model in LAC, the reform attempted to delegate to hospital management decision powers over the use of all resources (physical, financial, personnel, development, and contract negotiation with purchasers). Most countries have attempted to introduce some sort of autonomy for public hospitals, but few have succeeded. Good case studies of the complexity of introducing public hospital autonomy include Argentina, Uruguay, and Panama.

Argentina introduced public hospital autonomy in 1993. The regulation called for provinces, which are responsible for delivering publicly financed health services, to implement public hospital autonomy in their systems. The proposal was broad and unspecific. Salta, Mendoza, Rio Negro, and a few other provinces introduced differing degrees of hospital autonomy. Few of these experiments survived. Contracting out hospital management to the private sector for one hospital in Salta (Pérez 2002) provides an interesting example as it has been successful in terms of efficiency and consumer satisfaction, but the province has not yet been able to replicate the model for other hospitals. Lack of flexibility in personnel management has hampered hospital autonomy not only in the LAC region, but also in OECD countries (for example, the United Kingdom and New Zealand).

Uruguay began increasing public hospital autonomy in the late 1990s. Despite increased autonomy, particularly for the largest, most complex hospitals, managerial autonomy is still restricted to a small part of resource management decisions. Flexibility in managing personnel has been one of the most difficult changes to bring about.

The San Miguelito Hospital in Panama is a good case study of hospital autonomy and also direct community participation in hospital governance. Under this pilot experiment, the Ministry of Health delegated most decision rights to hospital management, even allowing a community not-for-profit foundation to manage the hospital directly. Opinions about the impact of this pilot on the population are mixed. Although the government and congress were able to pass all required legislation for this pilot, it encountered strong opposition, particularly from health sector unions. These difficulties suggest that the pilot could not easily be replicated and scaled up in Panama.

Other examples of direct community participation in provider governance and management include the CLAS pilot project with primary health care centers in Peru, with promising results (Harding and Alvarado 2005), and in Bolivia, the decentralization of oversight of primary health care centers decentralized to municipalities for the maternal and child health insurance program (Lavadenz 2001).

## Introducing Competition for Mandatory Health Insurance and Service Delivery

Many LAC countries included elements of public-private competition in their health systems during the 1990s. The most significant issues arising from these changes, which continue to be hotly debated even outside the LAC region, include demand-side subsidization of health insurance for the poor and private sector participation and public-private competition in the delivery of mandatory social health insurance. Chile and Colombia are the most pertinent examples of these reforms.

In a complete overhaul of its social security system in 1980, Chile reformed its social health insurance system, introducing private-public competition for mandatory health insurance. The reform allowed all formal workers, independently of their incomes, to choose between private health insurers (ISAPREs) and the public national health fund (FONASA) for their mandatory coverage. The reform mandated, however, that public subsidies would be given only to FONASA beneficiaries, irrespective of the income and risk profiles of people opting for ISAPREs. The reform greatly expanded both private health insurance coverage and private delivery of health services. It also resulted in severe segmentation of the risk pool with the high-income, low-risk affiliates concentrated in the ISAPRE system and the low-income, high-risk affiliates concentrated in FONASA.

Much has been written worldwide about the lessons of the Chilean reforms. Still, controversy swirls about the long-term impact of this segmentation on the poor and the determinants of such segmentation. This experiment yielded three main lessons about the crucial importance of strengthening regulatory capacity and shifting from traditional command and control to regulation and about the management of incentives when introducing private sector participation; the key role of public subsidies and risk-income equalization mechanisms to avoid segmentation and reduce or eliminate potentially negative effects on equity; and the enormous technical, political, and regulatory challenges that arise in developing countries attempting this type of reform.

In 1994, Colombia also introduced a radical reform of its SI for health (as well as old age pensions). Colombia's reforms followed along the lines of the Chilean reform of the 1980s in allowing all citizens to choose from among private health insurance administrators, including also the National Social Security Institute. However, the Colombian reform introduced more significant improvements than the Chilean reform of the 1980s. It introduced demand-side subsidization of insurance premiums for the poor, thus reducing a key factor that led to market segmentation by income in Chile. It also introduced an explicit BP and a risk-income equalization fund, both significantly reducing (but not yet eliminating) the incentives for risk-based market segmentation. These innovations are being gradually introduced in Chile following the Colombian experience.

The literature suggests that introducing private health insurance and competition in the insurance market can bring important benefits (Sheshinski and López-Calva 1998; Londoño and Frenk 1997) but also warns of problems that can arise from such reforms. Problems such as risk selection and "underservice" have been studied intensively (Arrow 1985; Laffont 1990; Milgrom and Roberts 1992; Hsiao 1994, 1995; Rothschild and Stiglitz 1976).

In the debate about whether harnessing private health insurance contributes to or impairs financial protection or health outcomes in LAC countries, the question is: Can countries take advantage of the benefits of health insurance competition but avoid the related efficiency and equity problems? At the core of the answer to this question is the technical and institutional issue of the feasibility of introducing specific financial, regulatory, and organizational reforms (for example, truncating the risk pyramid by creating a virtual single pool for costly, infrequent conditions; risk-adjustment mechanisms; risk-equalization and solidarity funds; and other mechanisms) (Baeza and Cabezas 1998; Newhouse 1998). And can this be done at transaction costs that would not offset the benefits of competition and privatization (Coase 1937; Williamson 1985)? In a competing, multiple insurance market, can countries reduce—or eliminate—risk selection, segmentation, and equity problems?

A vast literature refers to the effectiveness and the feasibility of implementing compensatory regulation, risk adjustment, and other mechanisms, most of it from OECD countries (Ellis et al. 1996; Ellis and van de Ven 1999; Newhouse 1998; Newhouse, Buntin, and Chapman 1997; Weiner et al. 1996). Evidence shows that, even with the inclusion of risk-equalization arrangements, the technical and institutional complexity of managing risk-adjustment mechanisms is high and costly. Even when some Latin American countries with coexisting organizational arrangements for risk pooling would benefit from some form of risk-adjustment system, it still remains to be seen whether the organizational and institutional capacity in most countries in the region would permit effective design and implementation of risk-adjustment mechanisms. There are two key examples of the introduction of private sector participation in mandatory risk pooling in the LAC region, Chile in 1985 (box 6.3) and Colombia in 1994.

---

**Box 6.3 Chile: The Challenge of Compensating for Market Failure in Health Insurance Competition**

In 1980, Chile implemented a radical reform of the health system along with structural reforms in the old-age pension system (Gill, Packard, and Yermo 2004). It divided financial administration in the public health sector between public providers and the MOH, creating the National Health Fund (FONASA), financed by a combination of general taxation (for the poor who are included in the pool) and a 7 percent payroll tax contribution from formal workers. Chile simultaneously allowed for the introduction of private competing health insurance organizations (ISAPREs). All workers and their families get to choose to contribute either to FONASA or an ISAPRE. In contrast with FONASA, which charges all members the same 7 percent payroll tax irrespective of risk, ISAPREs are allowed to adjust the contribution and the BP to reflect the risk of the principal and his or her family. Both organizational forms respond to different, opposing rationales. While FONASA is based on salary-related contributions with no exclusions, ISAPREs in practice are based on risk-related contributions. No regulatory agency, except for a very limited oversight by MOH, was set up to regulate ISAPREs until 10 years after their creation. Thus, for a long time, the stewardship function depended only on hierarchical, command-and-control external incentives—which proved ineffectual. As a result, ISAPREs grew from covering 2 percent of the population in 1983 to 27 percent in 1996.

Lack of regulation and weak stewardship resulted in a severe market segmentation. The ISAPREs focused on the richest affiliates and risk-selected the healthiest affiliates. The stewardship function did not begin to work until the late 1990s, and a regulation to reduce risk selection was introduced. All public subsidies to the poor and the high-risk population

*(Box continues on the following page.)*

*Box 6.3* (continued)

are channeled through FONASA to help reduce market segmentation. In the segmented market, although more than 9 percent of the population is older than 60 years (usually the highest risk population group), ISAPREs covered only about 3 percent of the over-60 population. At the same time, almost all low-income workers are in FONASA.

To correct this structural problem, Chile has begun an extensive reform of the health insurance system. Between 1999 and 2005, Chile introduced a mandatory BP, financial incentives, and major changes in the health insurance regulation—all in an attempt to correct these severe failures of health insurance competition.

*Source:* Adapted from WHO 2000.

## Lessons and Challenges

So far, there is little evidence of the impact of health sector reforms on health status, use of services, or financial protection in Latin America and the Caribbean. However, evidence beginning to emerge suggests some lessons from health system reform and efforts to improve financial protection through universal risk pooling. These lessons are closely interrelated:

- Fiscal sustainability is all important.
- Improvements are urgently needed in the performance-incentive framework for public providers along with civil service reform to increase provider autonomy in health personnel management.
- Private sector participation needs to be expanded in the delivery of publicly financed health services, as well as contributory risk pooling under an effective regulatory framework.

Reforms to improve fiscal sustainability and public provider performance face three main challenges: covering the growing numbers of informal sector workers; negotiating the political constraints on health sector reform; and strengthening technical, regulatory, and institutional capacity for complex and time-extensive reforms. Improving private sector participation also faces the challenge of technical and institutional capacity, but its success is closely linked to fiscal sustainability and changing the incentive framework for public providers. Under public providers, we include all providers usually owned and managed by the NHS and by social security organizations. The lessons and challenges discussed in this section are valid for both.

## The Lessons

*The imperative of ensuring fiscal sustainability* is a major lesson in LAC's experience with health sector reform. Fiscal sustainability has been an issue not only for extending effective risk pooling, but also for sustaining the substantial gains of the last two decades. Transitioning away from payroll tax and toward increasing the share of health service financed from general tax revenue will take a long time due to lagging tax-collection capacity and the complexity of pending tax reforms. During the transition, worker participation in contributory risk pooling needs to be expanded and efficiency increased in the delivery of publicly financed health services. The LAC experience shows that changing the incentive framework for public providers and improving private sector participation are the roots of efficiency gains.

*Improving the public provider incentive framework is essential for efficiency gains.* Current supply-side financing, based mostly on past budget expenditures, sets perverse incentives within the public health sector. Even worse, it virtually determines that public providers will capture public subsidies and allows policy makers little or no flexibility for reallocating resources to fit current and emerging epidemiological and financial protection needs. This capture also makes it all but impossible to contract out to private providers as needed, even when adequate public financing and regulatory framework are available.

As discussed also in chapter 4, both improving the incentive framework for public providers and improving private sector participation in health care requires the strengthening of strategic purchasing, particularly by introducing provider-payment mechanisms linked to the production of services rather than to historical budgets. This new provider-payment system is a prerequisite for a transition away from historical supply-side financing toward demand-side, or at least production-based, payment mechanisms for public providers. "Money should follow the patient" seems to be the rationale behind all internal market reforms discussed in this chapter. As envisioned in many of these reforms, a well-designed financing system would send public providers the right price signals and incentives to improve technical efficiency, increase productivity, and improve responsiveness to consumers. However, a resounding lesson of provider-payment reform in LAC is that public providers need flexibility to manage all production factors. They have to be able to adapt their service production functions and cost structures to the continuing evolution of the price signals determined by the new payment mechanisms so that they can compete among themselves and with private providers.

The average public provider in LAC spends 60 percent or more of its budgets on salaries, which makes human resources the prime production factor in health care delivery. Managers therefore need flexibility to allocate, hire, and fire their employees. To be successful, provider-payment reforms need to allow managers some autonomy to manage personnel as well as to solve other traditional public ownership constraints on effective management. Experience during the last 15 years shows that this change has not been easy. Labor market, medical labor market, and labor regulation reforms within the public health sector are key for effective strategic purchasing, but mostly missing from health sector reform agendas in the LAC region. Civil service reform lags notoriously behind the innovative and dynamic health financing reform efforts and is an area in which policy research and innovation are badly needed.

This lack of flexibility largely explains concerns about the potential fiscal impact of increasing public purchasing from private providers. Again, Chile's experience with FONASA and Colombia's with the Administradora de Régimen Subsidiado (ARS), as well as Brazil's apparently successful experience at the state level, deserve close examination. In the absence of incremental resources, shifting away from supply-side historical financing for public providers, using part of the budget to purchase from private providers, or forming other public providers, might generate deficits for public providers that lose revenue to their competitors. Even marginal deficits can unleash large disruptions. This would occur if the facility managers remain subject to rigid civil servant regulations for managing personnel that prevent them from adjusting the cost structure dynamically when demand for services slackens. Under such restrictions, deficits can occur.

Who ends up covering the deficits? Most likely the treasury (ministry of finance). Without flexibility to cut personnel or other costs to compensate for reduced revenue from the public purchaser, the public provider would have the same cost structure and would still have to pay people who cannot be transferred, laid-off, or in some cases, not even retrained. Lessons from Colombia's and Chile's experience in this regard are extremely valuable.

The initial provider-payment reforms and the increased selectivity of public purchasers in LAC have assumed that:

• Managers of public providers would receive and understand the price signals in the new payment mechanisms
• Managers would know how to respond and would act appropriately
• Managers would have the flexible, legal, and administrative environment allowing them to make the right changes
• Political authorities and the government would deal with the political problems associated with such flexibility.

Lessons from reform efforts in the LAC region have challenged all of these assumptions.

## The Challenges

The growing share of informal sector employment in LAC poses a significant challenge, not only to fiscal sustainability, but to the foundations of social health insurance (see chapter 5).

There are formidable obstacles to improving the incentive framework for public providers and expanding private sector participation. The introduction of labor flexibility and performance payments is rarely supported by health sector unions, usually the largest and most powerful public sector unions remaining after privatization of most public enterprises. For their part, influential private sector actors often interpret improvement of private sector participation as doing more of the same (much more). Improving private participation does mean doing more, but it also means enacting and enforcing effective regulations for private insurers and private providers—rarely supported by owners of private sector providers. Moreover, discussion of both issues is highly ideological and politicized. Reformers, with rare exceptions, have found these two challenges difficult to surmount. Instead of telling people what they will gain, reformers too often dwell on the technical and efficiency virtues of proposed changes and fail to win buy-in and support. As a result, voters frequently side with powerful public sector unions.

As evident from this report, health sector reforms in LAC are technically and institutionally demanding, and many of them are at the cutting edge of worldwide technical knowledge. This, coupled with a possible lack of in-country technical expertise and reform team continuity, poses momentous challenges. To succeed, health sector reform needs to be made a continuous national policy lasting from one administration to the next. Continuity in reform policy and execution has proven essential.

## Notes

1. See discussion below under Achieving Universal Coverage.

2. In 2005, the CFPGC covered only five services: treatment for cervix-uterine cancer, acute lymphoblastic leukemia, HIV-drugs, and neonatal intensive care for premature children with sepsis or hyaline membrane syndrome. However, it is intended to gradually incorporate more diseases using as inclusion criteria cost-effectiveness principles, social acceptability, as well as financial and infrastructure constraints.

3. Virtual single pool in the sense that although multiple organizations would coexist, all of them would be subject to the same rules regarding BP, portability, means-tested demand-side public subsidization of beneficiaries' premiums, minimum size, and other operational details.

# References

Araujo, A., and Bruno Funchal. 2005. "The Past and Future of Bankruptcy Law in Brazil and Latin America." São Paulo: Fundação Getúlio Vargas. Processed.

Arenas De Mesa, Alberto. 2000. "Cobertura previsional en Chile: lecciones y desafíos del sistema de pensiones administrado por el sector privado." Financiamiento del Desarrollo, No. 105. Santiago: Comisión Económica para America Latina (CEPAL).

Arrow, K. 1985. "Uncertainty and the Welfare Economics of Medical Care." In K.J. Arrow, ed., "Collected Papers of Kenneth J. Arrow," vol. 6, *Applied Economics*.

Atkinson, Antony B., and Joseph Stiglitz. 1980. *Lectures in Public Economics*. London and New York: McGraw-Hill.

Babu, B.V., A.N.Nayak, K.Dhal et al. 2002. "The Economic Loss Due to Treatment Costs and Work Loss to Individuals with Chronic Lymphatic Filariasis in Rural Communities of Orissa, India." Acta Tropica 82 (2002) 31–38.

Baeza, C. 1998. "Taking Stock of Health Sector Reform in Latin America: Trends and Challenges for Health Reform." Discussion Paper presented for the World Bank Development Week. Washington, D.C.: World Bank, Human Development Department, Latin America and the Caribbean Region.

Baeza, C. 2000. "Tendencia y desafíos en la seguridad social en salud." Congreso Anual de la Asociación Latinoamericana de Medicina Integral (ALAMI), Cartagena, Colombia.

Baeza, C. 2002. "Social Protection in Health." From materials in the Health Reform Course. Baltimore, Md.: Johns Hopkins University.

Baeza, C., and M. Cabezas. 1998. "La separación de funciones en la modernización del sector público de salud: Conceptos, avances y estado actual de experiencias internacionales representativas." Santiago de Chile: Centro Latinoamericano de Investigación de Sistemas de Salud (CLAISS).

———. 1999. "Is There a Need for Risk Adjustment in Health Insurance in Latin America?" Working Paper. Washington, D.C.: World Bank.

Baeza, C., and C. Copetta. 1999. "Análisis conceptual de la necesidad y factibilidad de introducir mecanismos de ajuste de riesgo en el contexto de portabilidad de los subsidios públicos en el sistema de seguros de salud en Chile." Santiago de Chile: Centro Latinoamericano de Investigación de Sistemas de Salud (CLAISS).

Baeza, C., F. Montenegro, and M. Núñez. 2002. "Extending Social Protection in Health through Community Based Health Organizations: Evidence and Challenges." Discussion Paper. Universitas Program—Strategies and Tools against Social Exclusion and Poverty (STEP). Geneva: International Labor Organization (ILO).

Baeza, C., P. Crocco, M. Núñez, and M. Shaffer. 2002. "Toward Decent Work: Social Protection in Health for All Workers and Their Families." Strategies and Tools against Social Exclusion and Poverty (STEP). Geneva: International Labor Organization (ILO).

Barr, N. 2001. "The Welfare State as Piggy Bank: Information, Risk, Uncertainty, and the Role of the State." Oxford, U.K.: Oxford University Press.

Bitran, R., and K. McInnes. 1993. "Demand for Health Care in Latin America: Lessons Drawn from the Dominican Republic and El Salvador." Edi Seminar Papers. Washington, D.C.: World Bank.

Bitran, R., U. Giedion, and R. Muñoz. 2004. "Fondos de riesgo, ahorro y prevención: estudio regional de políticas para la protección de los más pobres de los efectos de los choques de salud: Estudio de caso de Chile." Background paper for the regional study "Beyond Survival: Protecting Households from the Impoverishing Effects of Health Shocks." Santiago, Chile.

Blanc, P., L. Trupin, M. Eisner, G. Earnest, P. Katz, L. Israel, and E. Yelin. 2001. "The Work Impact of Asthma and Rhinitis: Findings from a Population-Based Survey." Journal of Clinical Epidemiology 54 (6): 610–8.

Blanchflower, D., and Andrew J. Oswald. 1991. "Self-Employment and Mrs. Thatcher's Enterprise Culture." Center for Economic Performance, Discussion Paper No. 30. London: London School of Economics.

Blau, David M. 1985. "Self-Employment and Self-Selection in Developing Country Labor Markets." Southern Economic Journal 51 (2): 351–63.

Boden, L. I., and M. Galizzi. 1999. "Economic Consequences of Workplace Injuries and Illnesses: Lost Earnings and Benefit Adequacy." American Journal of Industrial Medicine 36 (5): 487–503.

Bodger, K. 2002. "Cost of Illness of Crohn's Disease." Pharmacoeconomics 20 (10): 639–52.

Cisternas, M., P. Blanc, I. Yen, P. Katz, G. Earnest, M. Eisner, S. Shiboski, and E. Yelin. 2003. "A Comprehensive Study of the Direct and Indirect Costs of Adult Asthma." Journal of Allergy and Clinical Immunology 111 (6): 1212–18.

CMH (Commission on Macroeconomics and Health). 2002. "Macroeconomics and Health: Investing in Health for Economic Development." Report of the CMH. Geneva: CMH and World Health Organization.

Coase, R. 1937. "The Nature of the Firm." Económica (November): 386–495.

Coate, S. 1995. "Altruism, the Samaritan's Dilemma, and Government Transfer Policy." The American Economic Review, vol. 85, 46–57.

Corsetti, G. 1994. "An Endogenous Growth Model of Social Security and the Size of the Informal Sector." Revista de Análisis Económico 9 (1): 57–76.

Cortez, R. 1999. "Health and Productivity in Peru: Estimates by Gender and Region." Working Paper Series. Washington, D.C.: Inter-American Development Bank.

de Codes, J., T. D. Baker, and D. Schumann. 1988. "The Hidden Costs of Illness in Developing Countries." Research in Human Capital Development 5: 127–45.

de Ferranti, D., G. Perry, F. Ferreira, M. Walton. 2004. "Inequality in Latin America and the Caribbean." Washington, D.C.: World Bank.

de Ferranti, D., G. Perry, L. Servén et al. 2000. "Securing Our Future in a Global Economy." Latin American and Caribbean Studies. Viewpoint Series. Washington, D.C.: World Bank.

Deolalikar, A. B. 1988. "Nutrition and Labor Productivity in Agriculture: Estimates for Rural South India." Review of Economics and Statistics 70 (3): 406–13.

Dror, D., and M. Jacqier. 1999. "Micro-Insurance: Extending Health Insurance to the Excluded." International Social Security Review 52 (1): 71–97.

Ehrlich, Isaac, and Gary Becker. 1972. "Market Insurance, Self-Insurance, and Self-Protection." Journal of Political Economy 80: 623–48.

Ellis, R., and W. van de Ven. 1999. "Risk Adjustment in Competitive Health Plan Markets." Chapter 17 in *Handbook of Health Economics,* ed. A. Culyer and J. Newhouse, New York: Elsivier.

Ellis, R., G. Pope, L. Iezzoni, J. Ayanian, D. Bates, H. Burstin, and A. Ash. 1996. "Diagnosis-Based Risk Adjustment for Medicare Capitation Payments." *Health Care Financing Review* Spring 17 (3): 101–28.

Espinoza, C., M. Tokman, and J. Rodríguez. 2005. "Finanzas publicas de la reforma." *Desafios de la Reforma.* Santiago, Chile: Universidad Andrés Bello, Institute of Public Policy and Health Management.

Fernandez, J. M. 2004. Background note on Spain's health reform for the regional study, "Beyond Survival: Protecting Households from the Impoverishing Effects of Health Shocks." Washington, D.C.: World Bank.

Ferrando, J., C. Hernández, and W. Savedoff. 1999. "Productivity and Health Status in Nicaragua." Working Paper Series. Washington, D.C.: Inter-American Development Bank.

Fiedler, J. 2004. "Out-of-Pocket Health Expenditures, Risk Pooling, Savings, and Prevention: A Honduras Case Study." Background Paper. Washington, D.C.: World Bank.

Fiorito, Riccardo, and Flavio Padrini. 2001. "Distortionary Taxation and Labor Market Performance." *Oxford Bulletin of Economics and Statistics* 63 (2): 173–96.

Gertler, P., and J. Gruber. 2002. "Insuring Consumption against Illness." *American Economic Review* 92 (1): 51–76.

Gertler, P., and J. Van der Gaag. 1988. "Willingness to Pay for Social Services in Developing Countries." LSMS Working Paper. Washington, D.C.: World Bank.

Gill, I., and N. Ilahi. 2000. "Economic Insecurity, Individual Behavior, and Social Policy." Background Paper for the Regional Study on Economic Insecurity. Washington, D.C.: World Bank, Office of the Chief Economist, Latin America and the Caribbean.

Gill, I., T. Packard, and J. Yermo. 2004. "Keeping the Promise of Social Security in Latin America." Palo Alto, Calif. World Bank and Stanford University Press.

Gordon, D. 2002. "The Dynamics of Poverty: Social Omnibus or Underclass Wagon?" Bristol, UK: Towsend Centre for International Poverty Research.

Guiso, L., and M. Paiella. 2000. "Risk Aversion, Wealth, and Financial Markets Imperfections." Working Paper. Rome: Ente Luigi Einaudi for Monetary, Banking, and Financial Studies and the Bank of Italy Research Development.

Gunderson, M., and D. Hyatt. 2000. "Workers' Compensation: Foundations for Reform." Toronto: University of Toronto Press.

Guyatt, G., D. Cook, and B. Haynes. 2004. "Evidence-based Medicine Has Come a Long Way." *BMJ 2004* 329: 990–91.

Harding, A., and B. Alvarado. 2005. "Primary Health Care and the CLAS in Peru: Background Paper for RECURSO Study." Washington, D.C.: World Bank.

Heffley, D., and T. Miceli. 1998. "The Economics of Incentive-Based Health Care Plans." *Journal of Risk and Insurance* 65 (3): 445–65.

Himmelstein, D., Deborah Thorne, Elizabeth Warren, and Steffie Woolhandler. 2005. "Illness and Injury as Contributors to Bankruptcy." *Journal Health Affairs*, February 2 (web edition).

Hirshleifer, J., and J. Riley. 1979. "The Analytics of Uncertainty and Information—An Expository Survey." *Journal of Economic Literature* 17: 1375–1421.

Holzmann, Robert, Truman Packard, and José Cuesta. 2000. "Extending Coverage in Multi-Pillar Pension Systems: Constraints, Hypotheses, Preliminary Evidence and Future Research Agenda." Social Protection Working Paper, No. 0002. Washington, D.C.: World Bank.

Hsiao, W. 1994. "Marketization—The Illusory Magic Pill." *Health Economics* 3: 351–57.

———. 1995. "Abnormal Economics in the Health Sector." *Health Policy* 32: 125–39.

IADB (Inter-American Development Bank). 2001. "Health Services in Latin America and Asia." Part 2. Baltimore, Md.: Johns Hopkins University Press.

James, E. 1999. "Coverage under Old Age Security Systems and Protection for the Uninsured: What Are the Issues?" Presentation given at Inter-American Development Bank conference on Social Protection, Washington, D.C.

Jayawardene, R. 1993. "Illness Perception: Social Cost and Coping-Strategies of Malaria Cases." *Social Science & Medicine* 37 (9): 1169–76.

Knaul, F. 1999. "Linking Health, Nutrition, and Wages: The Evolution of Age at Menarche and Labor Earnings among Adult Mexican Women." Working Paper Series. Washington, D.C.: Inter-American Development Bank.

Knaul, F., H. Arreola, O. Mendez, and V. Leyva. 2004. "Catastrophic and Impoverishing Health Expenditure: Increasing Risk Pooling in the Mexican Health System." Background paper for the regional study "Beyond Survival: Protecting Households from the Impoverishing Effects of Health Shocks." Washington, D.C.: World Bank.

Knight, F. 1921. "Risk, Uncertainty, and Profit." New York: Houghton-Miffin.

Kutzin, J. 2000. "Towards Universal Coverage: A Goal-oriented Framework for Policy Analysis." HNP Discussion Paper. Washington, D.C.: World Bank.

———. 2001. "A Descriptive Framework for Country-level Analysis of Health Care Financing Arrangements." *Health Policy* 56 (2001): 171–204.

Laffont, J. 1979. *Aggregation and Revelation of Preferences*, New York: Elsevier North-Holland, 11.

———. 1990. "The Economics of Uncertainty and Information." Cambridge, Mass.: MIT Press.

Lavadenz, F. 2001. "Basic Health Insurance in Bolivia: An Instrument to Increase Equity and Health Care Access for the Poor." In *Health Services in Latin America and Asia*, ed. C. Molina and J. Nunez del Arco, Washington, D.C.: Inter-American Institute for Social Development.

Lederer, P., D. Weltle, and A. Weber. 2001. "Illness-Related Premature Unfitness for Work among Civil Servants in Bavaria—An Evaluation in the Social Medical Field." *Gesundheitswesen* 63 (8–9): 509–13.

Lenz, R., F. Volante, and O. Arteaga. 2004. "Políticas Pro-Pobre en el Sector público de Salud del Perú: Cúales son los Próximos pasos?" Background paper for the RECURSO Peru Study. Washington, D.C.: World Bank.

Londoño, J. 1996. "Estructurando pluralismo en los servicios de salud: la experiencia colombiana." *Revista de Análisis Económico* 11 (2): 37–60.

Londoño, J., and J. Frenk. 1997. "Structured Pluralism: Toward an Innovative Model for Health System Reform in Latin America." *Health Policy* 41 (1): 1–36.

Maceira, D. 2004. "Mecanismos de protección social en salud e impacto de shocks financieros: El caso de Argentina." Background paper for the regional study "Beyond Survival: Protecting Households from the Impoverishing Effects of Health Shocks." Washington, D.C.: World Bank.

Maloney, W. 1998a. "The Structure of the Labor Market in Developing Countries: Time Series Evidence and Competing Views." Policy Research Working Paper No. 1940. Washington D.C.: World Bank.

———. 1998b. "Are Labor Markets in Developing Countries Dualistic?" Policy Research Working Paper No. 1941. Washington D.C.: World Bank.

———. 2000. "Minimum Wages in Latin America: A Note." Washington D.C.: World Bank, Poverty Reduction and Economic Management Department.

————. 2004. "Informality Revisited." *World Development* 32 (7): 1159–78.

Marshall, J. R. 1976. "Moral Hazard." *American Economic Review* 66: 880–90.

Maynard, A. 1994. "Can Competition Enhance Efficiency in Health Care? Lessons from the Reform of the UK National Health Service." *Social Science & Medicine* 39 (10): 1433–45.

Milgrom, P., and J. Roberts. 1992. "Economics, Organization and Management." Englewood Cliffs, N.J.: Prentice Hall.

Mills, A. 1994. "The Economic Consequences of Malaria for Households: A Case-Study in Nepal." *Health Policy* 29 (3): 209–27.

Mock, C., S. Gloyd, S. Adjei, F. Acheampong, and O. Gish. 2003. "Economic Consequences of Injury and Resulting Family Coping Strategies in Ghana." *Accident Analysis and Prevention* 35 (1): 81–90.

Montenegro, F. 2004. "Household Health Expenditures, Financial Protection, and Poverty in Ecuador." Background paper for the regional study "Beyond Survival: Protecting Households from the Impoverishing Effects of Health Shocks." Washington, D.C.: World Bank.

Montenegro, F., and R. Nazerali. 2004. "Health and Household Income and Consumption: A Review of the Literature." Background Paper. Washington, D.C.: World Bank.

Mossialos, E., A. Dixon, J. Figueras, and J. Kutzin. 2002. *Funding Health Care: Options for Europe.* Berkshire: Open University Press.

Murrugarra, E., and M. Valdivia. 1999. "The Returns to Health for Peruvian Urban Adults: Differentials across Genders, the Life-Cycle and the Wage Distribution." Working Paper Series. Washington, D.C.: Inter-American Development Bank.

Musgrove, P. 1996. "Un fundamento conceptual para el rol público y privado en la salud." *Análisis Económico* 11 (2): 9–36.

Neuhauser, F., and S. Raphael. 2004. "The Effect of an Increase in Workers' Compensation Benefits on the Duration and Frequency of Benefit Receipt." *Review of Economics and Statistics* 86 (1): 288–302.

Newhouse, J. P. 1998. "Risk Adjustment: Where Are We Now?" *Inquiry* 35 (2): 122–31.

Newhouse, J., M. Buntin, and J. Chapman. 1997. "Risk Adjustment and Medicare: Taking a Closer Look." *Health Affairs* 16 (3): 26–43.

OECD (Organisation for Economic Co-operation and Development). 1992. *The Reform of Health Care: A Comparative Analysis of Seven OECD Countries.* Health Policy Studies. Paris: OECD.

Packard, T. 2002a. "Pooling, Savings, and Prevention: Mitigating the Risk of Old Age Poverty in Chile." World Bank Policy Research Working Paper No. 2849. Washington, D.C.: World Bank.

————. 2002b. "Are There Positive Incentives from Privatizing Social Security? A Panel Analysis of Pension Reforms in Latin America." *Journal of Pension Economics and Finance* 1 (2): 89–109.

————. 2005. "Household Risk Management and Social Protection in Chile." World Bank Country Study. Washington, D.C.: World Bank.

Packard, T., and A. Barr. 2002a. "Preferences, Constraints, and Substitutes for Coverage under Peru's Pension System." Background paper for regional study on social security reform. Washington, D.C.: World Bank, Office of the Chief Economist, Latin America and the Caribbean Region.

————. 2002b. "Revealed Preference and Self-Insurance: Can We Learn from the Self-Employed in Chile?" World Bank Policy Research Working Paper No. 2754. Washington, D.C.: World Bank.

PAHO (Pan American Health Organization). 2002. *Health in the Americas 2002 Edition.* vol. 2. Washington, D.C.: PAHO.

Parker, S. 1999. "Elderly Health and Salaries in the Labor Market." Working Paper Series. Inter-American Development Bank: Washington, D.C.

Pauly, M. 1986. "Taxation, Health Insurance, and Market Failure in the Medical Economy." *Journal of Economic Literature* 24 (2): 629–75.

Peabody, J. W., S. W. Lee, S. R. Bickel. 1995. "Health for All in the Republic of Korea: One Country's Experience with Implementing Universal Health Care," *Health Policy*, 31 (January 1995): 29–42.

Pérez, L. 2002. "Hospital governance in Argentina." Background paper for a regional study on hospital governance in Argentina, Brazil, Colombia, and Mexico. Buenos Aires. Processed.

Phelps, C. E. 1978. "Illness Prevention and Medical Insurance." Supplement: National Bureau of Economic Research Conference on the Economics of Physician and Patient Behavior. *Journal of Human Resources* 13 (Suppl.): 183–207.

Pradhan, M., and N. Prescott. 2002. "Social Risk Management Options for Medical Care in Indonesia." *Health Economics* 11: 431–46.

Preker, A. S., and J. Langenbrunner. 2005. "Spending Wisely: Buying Health Services for the Poor." Washington, D.C.: World Bank.

Principi, N., S. Esposito, P. Marchisio, R. Gasparini, and P. Crovari. 2003. "Socioeconomic Impact of Influenza on Healthy Children and Their Families." *Journal of Pediatric Infectious Diseases* 22 (10 Suppl.): S207–10.

Restrepo, M. 1996. "La reforma a la Seguridad Social en Salud de Colombia y la teoría de la competencia regulada." Paper prepared for the Comisión Económica para America Latina. Bogotá, Colombia: CEPAL.

Ribero, R., and J. Nuñez. 1999. "Productivity of Household Investment in Health: The Case of Colombia." Working Paper Series. Washington, D.C.: Inter-American Development Bank.

Robinson, R., and J. Le Grand. 1994. "Evaluating the National Health Service Reforms." Policy Journals. Oxford: Transaction Books.

Rofman, R. 2003. "El Sistéma Provisional y la Crisis en la Argentina." Documento de Trabajo, February 2003. Washington, D.C.: World Bank.

Rothschild, M., and J. Stiglitz. 1976. "Equilibrium in Competitive Insurance Markets: An Essay on the Economics of Imperfect Information." *Quarterly Journal of Economics* 90 (4): 630–49.

Sackett, D. L., W. M. Rosenberg, J. A. Gray, R. B. Haynes, and W. S. Richardson. 1996. "Evidence-Based Medicine: What It Is and What It Isn't." *BMJ 1996* 312: 71–2.

Sauerborn, R., I. Ibrango, A. Nougtara, M. Borchert, M. Hien, J. Benzler, E. Koob, and H. Diesfeld. 1995. "The Economic Costs of Illness for Rural Households in Burkina Faso." *Tropical Medicine and Parasitology* 46 (1): 54–60.

Savedoff, William. 2004. "Tax-Based Financing for Health Systems: Options and Experience." Health Financing Issues Paper (EIP/FER/HFP/PIP.04.4). Geneva: World Health Organization, Department of Health Systems Financing, Expenditure, and Resource Allocation.

Savedoff, W. D., and T. P. Schultz. 2000. "Wealth from Health: Linking Social Investments to Earnings in Latin America." Washington, D.C.: Inter-American Development Bank.

Schieber, G., C. Baeza, D. Kress, and M. Maier. 2006. "Financing Health Systems in the 21st Century." In *Disease Control Priorities in Developing Countries*, (2nd edition), 225–42. New York: Oxford University Press.

Schmidt-Hebbel, K., and Luis Servén. 1996. "Hacia una menor Inflación en Chile: Contracción monetaria bajo expectativas racionales." In *Análisis empirico de la inflación en Chile*, ed. F. Morande and F. Rosende. Santiago de Chile: ILADES and Pontificia Universidad Católica de Chile.

Sheshinski, E., and L. López-Calva. 1998. "Privatization and Its Benefits: Theory and Evidence." Cambridge, Mass.: Harvard University. Processed.

Smith, L., D. Romero, P. Word, N. Wampler, W. Chavkin, and P. Wise. 2002. "Employment Barriers among Welfare Recipients and Applicants with Chronically Ill Children." *American Journal of Public Health* 92 (9): 1453–57.

Stewart, W., J. Ricci, E. Chee, D. Morgastein, and R. Lipton. 2003. "Lost Productive Time and Cost Due to Common Pain Conditions in the US Workforce." *Journal of the American Medical Association* 290 (18): 2443–54.

Summers, L. 1989. "Some Simple Economics of Mandated Benefits." *AEA Papers and Proceedings* 79 (2): 177–183.

Taylor, M. 1996. "Earnings, Independence or Unemployment: Why Become Self-Employed?" *Oxford Bulletin of Economics and Statistics* 58 (2): 253–65.

Tokman, M., J. Rodríguez, and F. Larraín. 2004. "Subsidio por incapacidad laboral 1991–2002: Incentivos institucionales, crecimiento del gasto y una propuesta de racionalización." *Estudios Públicos* 934 (2004): 12–14.

Torche, Aristides, and Gert Wagner. 1997. "Previsión social: valoración individual de un beneficio mandatado." *Cuadernos de Economía* No. 103, PUCC.

UNDP (United Nations Development Programme). 2004. *Human Development Report 2004*. New York: UNDP.

Uusitalo, R. 1999. "Homo Entreprenaurus?" Working Paper No. 205. Helsinki: Government Institute for Economic Research.

Valdes, S. 2002. "Social Security Coverage in Chile, 1990–2001." Background paper for regional study on social security reform. Washington, D.C.: World Bank, Office of the Chief Economist, Latin America and the Caribbean Region.

Vijverberg, Wim P. M. 1986. "Consistent Estimates of the Wage Equation When Individuals Choose among Income-Earning Activities." *Southern Economic Journal* 52 (April): 1028–42.

Wagstaff, A., and M. Pradhan. 2003. "Evaluating the Impacts of Health Insurance: Looking Beyond the Negative." Policy Research Paper. Washington, D.C.: World Bank.

Weiner, J., A. Dobson, S. Maxwell, K. Coleman, B. Starfield, and G. Anderson. 1996. "Risk-Adjusted Medicare Capitation Rates Using Ambulatory and Inpatient Diagnoses." *Health Care Financing Review* 17 (3): 77–99.

WHO (World Health Organization). 2000. *World Health Report 2000—Health Systems: Improving Performance*. Geneva: WHO.

———. 2004. *World Health Report 2004—Changing History*. Geneva: WHO.

Williamson, O. 1985. *The Economic Institutions of Capitalism*. New York: Free Press.

World Bank. 1994. "Averting the Old Age Crisis: Policies to Protect the Old and Promote Growth." World Bank Policy Research Report. New York: Oxford University Press.

———. 1997. "UK Study Tour: Back to Office Report." Office Memorandum. Washington, D.C.: World Bank. Processed.

———. 2002. *Revised HNP Strategy Paper*. Washington, D.C.: World Bank.

———. 2003. *World Development Indicators 2003*. Washington D.C.: World Bank.

———. 2004a. "Country Assistance Strategy for the Republic of Costa Rica." Report No. 28570. Washington, D.C.: World Bank.

———. 2004b. "Averting the Old Age Crisis: Policies to Protect the Old and Promote Growth." World Bank Policy Research Report. New York: Oxford University Press.

———. 2004c. "Project Appraisal Document on a Proposed Loan for a Health Transition Project in Support of the First Phase of the Program for Transformation in Health." Report No. 27717-TU. Washington, D.C.: World Bank, Human Development Unit, Europe and Central Asia Region.

———. 2005. *World Development Indicators 2005*. Washington, D.C.: World Bank.

Yamada, G. 1996. "Urban Informal Employment and Self-Employment in Developing Countries: Theory and Evidence." *Economic Development and Cultural Change* 44: 289–314.

# Index